Copyright © 2000 by Mark Gauvreau Judge

All rights reserved. No part of this publication may be reproduced or transmitted in any form or by any means, electronic or mechanical, including photocopy, recording, or any information storage and retrieval system now known or to be invented, without permission in writing from the publisher, except by a reviewer who wishes to quote brief passages in connection with a review written for inclusion in a magazine, newspaper, or broadcast.

Published in the United States by
Spence Publishing Company
111 Cole Street
Dallas, Texas 75207

Library of Congress Cataloging-in-Publication Data

Judge, Mark Gauvreau, 1964-
    If it ain't got that swing : the rebirth of grown-up culture / by Mark Gauvreau Judge
        p. cm.
    Includes bibliographical references and index.
    ISBN 1-890626-24-4 (hardcover)
    1. United States—Civilization—1945-. 2. United States—Social conditions—1980-. 3. Popular culture—United States—History—20th century. 4. Swing (Dance)—United States—History. 5. Adulthood—Social aspects—United States—History—20th century. 6. Suburbs—United States—History—20th century. 7. City and town life—United States—History—20th century.
    E169.12 .J83 2000
    973.92—dc21   00-026706

Printed in the United States of America

To

Duke Ellington

Contents

Illustrations

Acknowledgments

THIS BOOK WOULD NOT HAVE BEEN POSSIBLE without the following people: Phyllis Mitchell Judge, a benefactor of the arts who offered more than I can adequately describe to support this project. Second and third are Russ Smith and John Strausbaugh, editor-in-chief and editor, respectively, of the *New York Press*. I was at the point of giving up on American newspapers, with their cardboard editorials and by-the-numbers cultural criticism, when I discovered the *New York Press*. I found there a place where writers with the kinds of voices and opinions that don't get past the gatekeepers of the mainstream and "alternative" press are welcomed and encouraged. Many of the pieces on swing that I first wrote for the *Press* became part of this book. I would never have completed it without them.

Other papers and magazines which ran pieces that became part of this book are the *Washington Post* (special thanks to Steve Luxenberg), *First Things* (whose editor, Richard John Neuhaus, is an inspiration), the *Weekly Standard* (thanks to J. Bottum), and the *Washington Times*. A special thanks is in order as well to the park staff, dancers, and musicians of Glen Echo.

Finally, I must acknowledge the vision and hard work of publisher Thomas Spence and editor Mitchell Muncy. This work, and others by people far wiser than I am, would never have been published without them.

ONE

The Secret City

Duke Ellington, the pride of Shaw.

Gordon Parks / The Library of Congress

ON A CLEAR AND UNUSUALLY MILD Saturday afternoon in February 1999, a group of about twenty people got together in Washington, D.C., to talk about what has gone wrong with the world.

"Kids have no discipline today," said a short, heavyset man in his sixties. "When I was growing up, everyone within a five-mile radius knew who I was. If I did anything wrong, it got back to my mother before I did. I'd get two beatings: one from the neighbor who caught me, then one from my mom."

"Amen," agreed a man in his fifties. "We couldn't even speak at the dinner table when I was a kid. You were home at dark, or you didn't get dinner and were sent to bed."

"The family was your center," offered a forty-year-old woman. "It was where you learned how to act."

"You couldn't go out on the street unless you were dressed right," piped in another man. "There was no such thing as 'homeless.'" He spat the word with disgust.

These people had gathered at Howard University, Washington's famous black university, for "I Remember U," a "tellabration," part of an oral history project of the Historical Society of Washington, D.C. Their task was to tell for reporters and guests what life was like between 1920 and 1960 in Shaw, Washington's most famous black neighborhood. For several hours, their laughter and memories filled the small classroom as they described a world that has become foreign.

Although it's not widely remembered, black Washington from 1920 to 1960 was a financial, spiritual, and cultural stronghold. Because Washington was a segregated city, blacks simply created their own metropolis. Just down the street from where we sat, jazz master Duke Ellington, born in Washington and raised in Shaw, had played his first gig. The first black bank, the Industrial Savings Bank, was started here. The black population of New York's Harlem inherited many of its buildings from previous white owners, but many of the buildings in Shaw were paid for by black businessmen and built by black hands: the True Reformers Building, the Laborers Building and Loan Association, the Whitelaw Hotel, the Twelfth Street YMCA, and the Prince Hall Lodge.

Shaw's schools and businesses were first-rate: at one time, Howard University, which H. L. Mencken called the black Sorbonne, was graduating 90 percent of the black doctors and half of the black lawyers in America. Many of Howard's students came from the nearby schools, which had a level of quality almost unimaginable today. The same week as the tellabration, the cultural ethic that once existed in Shaw was nicely summed up by *Washington Post* columnist Courtland Milloy in a piece about Evelyn B. Granville, a seventy-four-year-old black physicist. Granville had been born in Washington in 1924 and attended the all-black Dunbar high school in Shaw before going to Smith College and Yale. Granville was returning to Washington to be honored for her accomplishments by the National Academy of Sciences and Dow Chemical. Though Milloy might have offered a sermon on overcoming Jim Crow, he sounded like William Bennett: "[Granville] represents something of an educational paradox: Born in the District in 1924, she grew up in an era characterized by some of the worst race relations in American history. . . . And yet, she recalls being immersed in a 'culture of learning,' where 'the colored schools of Washington, D.C., were privileged to have well-trained and dedicated teachers.'"

They were also teachers who weren't afraid to discipline their students. One of the reccurring themes of the tellabration was that children today are out of control. "If you ever did anything against the teacher," said one man at the Howard meeting, "your parents immediately took the teacher's side. It was them against you, unlike today, when the parents never admit their kid does anything wrong and everyone sues each other." The man sitting next to him offered his own story: "My job was to sweep off the porch before my mom got home from work. I'll never forget the day I didn't do it. I heard my mom come up the front porch and say, 'I must be imagining things. I swear, I must be losing my mind. I could have sworn I told somebody to sweep this porch.' I'll never forget hearing her come up those stairs."

Only a few blocks north of the White House and in the shadow of Griffith Stadium, where the Washington Senators and the Negro League's Homestead Grays played baseball, Shaw was like a foreign capital that had been surreptitiously placed in the nation's capital. "You'd save up all week to take the trolley into Shaw and U Street," one middle-aged woman recalled. "It was like going to a European city. We had everything there." U Street, Shaw's famous main thoroughfare, boasted over three hundred black-owned businesses. Black doctors, lawyers, dentists, photographers, and pharmacists competed for space with jazz clubs like the Bohemian Caverns, Republic Gardens, the Cavern Club, and the Club Bengasi, as well as theaters, churches, and social and dance halls. Churches were essential social and spiritual centers— the only establishments open on Sunday.

A 1932 article in *Crisis* magazine, the organ of the NAACP, referred to Shaw as "the secret city," for its invisibility to white Washington. Albert Murray described Shaw in a piece in the *Nation*, published around the time of the tellabration: "The Washington of [the 1920s] . . . was not provincial in matters of entertainment and the arts. It was not as cosmopolitan as New York, to be sure, but even so, it reflected much of the New Yorker's taste, perhaps comparable to a suburb of Manhattan." People dressed well when they went out in Shaw. As one man observed, "you couldn't walk down the street without a tie." In ways unimaginable today, it was safe. "You never locked your doors," one tellabrator recalled. "You just walked out. I could go to the Industrial Bank and cash a one-hundred-dollar check and come out with all the money exposed in my hand and wouldn't even think of somebody snatching it. That's the kind of comfort you had." Another called the atmosphere "busy, happy-go-lucky, bustling, safe," adding that he "was on U Street every day, every night, until two o'clock in the morning."

⌇

I HAD COME TO THE TELLABRATION for three related reasons: the abandonment of my radicalism, Duke Ellington, and swing dancing.

I arrived at young adulthood a radical leftist, steeped in the counterculture of the 1960s and the rock 'n' roll nihilism of the 1990s. My life on the left began while I was in college, during the presidency of Ronald Reagan. My father had worked in the Kennedy Administration, and though I absorbed some of my political opinions from him, we had crucial differences. The New Deal liberalism Dad had grown up with sought to help people while retaining many of the Victorian values that held American culture together. One could be a New Dealer and believe in religion, morality, and the proper way to dress when you left the house. My father disliked Republicans, but also believed abortion is murder.

For my part, I completely absorbed the New Left liberalism of the 1960s. I believed that America was a country club filled with bigoted neanderthals pushing an atavistic cultural agenda and supporting unworkable and cruel eco-

nomic theories. I believed this, moreover, without knowing
anything about economics and even less about human nature. I grew my hair long, renounced my Catholicism to
champion atheism, worshiped rock 'n' roll as the music of
revolution, and went to protest rallies. I told myself I was full
of compassion: I felt for the poor victims of Reaganism, the
people bombed in America's imperialist wars, and poor mil-
lionaire rockers "censored" by having to put a warning sticker
on their product.

Now I can't remember the motivation for my radicalism,
other than the desire for attention. (Narcissism has afflicted
the left for forty years.) Or maybe it was genetic: my dad once
laughingly said that I was "crazy" from the time I appeared
in the delivery room. I do know why I changed; I remember
the exact moment. It was the winter of 1994, and I was reading *The Revolt of the Elites and the Betrayal of Democracy*, the
last book by the late historian and social critic Christopher
Lasch, when I came across this passage:

> The ideology of compassion, however agreeable to our
> ears, is one of the principal influences ... of the subver-
> sion of civic life, which depends not so much on com-
> passion as on mutual respect. A misplaced compassion
> degrades both the victims, who are reduced to objects
> of pity, and their would-be benefactors, who find it
> easier to pity their fellow citizens than to hold them up
> to impersonal standards, attainment of which would
> entitle them to respect. We pity those who suffer, and

we pity, most of all, those who suffer conspicuously; but we reserve respect for those who refuse to exploit their suffering for the purposes of pity.

For the first time in years, I experienced political self-doubt. I had been living in a fortress of liberal self-righteousness, but Lasch had managed to breach the wall.

Shortly after I read Lasch, I became interested in jazz music. I was particularly taken by the songs of Duke Ellington, one of the greatest composers America has ever produced. The genius behind "Mood Indigo," "In a Sentimental Mood," "I'm Beginning to See the Light," "C-Jam Blues," and hundreds of other classic Ellington songs, was an elegant, articulate, stylish, patrician who had grown up the son of a butler and risen to play for presidents. What many people don't know is that Ellington acquired his grace and élan in Shaw. He was born poor and black in 1899 and was raised during one of the worst periods of racism in American history. According to my leftist logic, he should have been so twisted with rage at his country that he couldn't get out of bed in the morning. It soon became obvious to me that Ellington would have thought of radical politics as a way for the less sophisticated to deal with their problems. Ellington didn't toss bricks; instead, he presented himself as everything that many white Americans weren't—swank, worldly, debonair— in short, a gentleman.

In his memoir, *Music Is My Mistress*, Ellington recalled that his father, a butler, drilled into him the importance of speaking well and carrying himself with dignity and aplomb no matter how poor he was. Ellington also recalled what he was taught at Garrison Public High School in Shaw, which he attended from 1908 to 1913:

> In addition to arithmetic, algebra, history, and English, which were taught as the most vital things in the world, my teacher—Miss Boston, the principal of the school —would explain the importance of proper speech. It would be most important in our lives to come. When we went out into the world, we would have the grave responsibility of being practically always on stage, for every time people saw a Negro they would go into a reappraisal of the race. She taught us that proper speech and good manners were our first obligations, because as representatives of the Negro race we were to command respect for our people. This being an all-colored school, Negro history was crammed into the curriculum, so that we would know our people all the way back. They had pride there, the greatest race pride, and at that time there was some kind of movement to desegregate the schools in Washington, D.C. Who do you think were the first to object? Nobody but the proud Negroes of Washington, who felt that the kind of white kids we would be thrown in with weren't good enough.

As a young man, Ellington's favorite places to hang out were Frank Holliday's, a pool hall, and the Howard Theatre, which was right next door. Many of the men who came into Holliday's had come from gigs at the Howard. It was from talents like Lester Dishman, Phil Wird, and Carolynne Thornton that Ellington learned his way around a piano. When he got his first job in a band, Ellington imitated Luckey Roberts, whom he had seen at the Howard. Ellington met his first drummer, Sonny Greer, through a mutual friend who played the theater.

The Howard was a place unlike any other. Before it was built in 1910 by black furniture store owner Benjamin Benedict (who realized that a black theater in a city without one was a sure money maker), there were no large black theaters in the country. In Washington, blacks were barred from downtown theaters like the Earle and the Fox . When the new fifteen-hundred-seat Howard went up on T Street in Shaw, it was a powerful symbol of black equality. Indeed, through the 1960s—with only a short closing during the Depression— the Howard offered a stunning list of talent: Ellington, Count Basie, Ella Fitzgerald, the Supremes, crooner and Washingtonian Billy Eckstine, and Charlie Parker (who refused to do an encore after a ten-minute ovation because he was sore at having to open for the D.C. rhythm-and-blues band the Clovers). In the 1950s, Sidney Poitier starred in an all-black version of "Detective Story." It would be easier to name the great black artists who didn't play the Howard—if there were any. For much of the early part of the century—and for decades before New York's Apollo desegregated in 1935—the

Howard was America's most potent and resplendent repudiation of racism.

On opening night in 1910, the black newspaper the *Washington Bee* reported, "Washington Society was out in full force . . . the private boxes were filled with many ladies of society." Present were "the social elite of Washington, gorgeously dressed in gowns fit for goddesses." The theater resembled a baroque palace, complete with crystal chandeliers, marble staircases, and eight proscenium boxes. Assistant U.S. Attorney J. A. Cobb and the ex-governor of Louisiana attended. The audience enjoyed European acrobats, German comedians, a minstrel group, and singer-actress Abbie Mitchell, who, the *Washington Bee* reported, "carried the house by storm."

Shaw and the Howard were precursors of and major contributors to the Harlem Renaissance of the 1920s. An efflorescence of intellectual and artistic creativity in New York following World War I, the Harlem Renaissance had as its aim the creation of equality through artistic achievement. James Weldon Johnson proclaimed that "the status of the Negro in the United States is more a question of national mental attitude toward the race than actual conditions. And nothing will do more to change that mental attitude and change his status than a demonstration of intellectual parity by the Negro through the production of literature and art."

Well before the Harlem Renaissance, U Street was known as "the black Broadway," home to the Black Theater Owners

Booking Association and the Colored Actors Union. There were ornate theaters on every corner: the Republic, the Booker T. Washington, and the Dunbar, named after the great black poet who had grown up in Washington. At the Lincoln Theatre on U Street, people could see a show, then go dancing at the Collonade, a ballroom in the same building. On Saturday nights after the last show let out, U Street would be jammed with thousands of well-dressed people drifting to clubs and restaurants. The Howard hosted lectures by figures such as Booker T. Washington. A 1916 Howard production called *Darktown Follies* would eventually make its way to Harlem, where it would become a smash. Langston Hughes lived at the Whitelaw Hotel on Thirteenth Street. Harlem Renaissance literary figure Jean Toomer was a Washingtonian who started as an assistant manager at the Howard.

Today the Howard is silent and falling apart, a victim of the moral and cultural collapse of the last forty years. It is all too emblematic of the decay of Shaw and other urban areas. After reading Ellington's account of the era and listening to the tellabrators recall the glories of the neighborhood, I couldn't believe that people had once been more afraid to walk the streets of Shaw without a tie than they were of being robbed. While some restaurants and clubs still struggle to make it, there is fresh paint on some houses, and the Lincoln Theater has been restored, much of Shaw—like America—is in dire need of rejuvenation. Vacant lots are common. Homeless men and drug dealers warm themselves on oil drum fires in front of the vacant and fire-damaged Dunbar Theater at Seventh and U, once one of the most vibrant corners of Shaw.

⌖

WHAT WENT WRONG? Most liberals point either to racism, which caused white flight from the city in the 1960s, or to the civil rights laws of the 1960s, which allowed blacks to go to theaters downtown and live in the suburbs—and thus started a flight from the city. But what truly plunged Washington into a dark age were the 1968 riot following the death of Martin Luther King, the arrival of the drug trade, and a collapse of morals. Almost overnight, the area around the Howard, once the stylish hub of the black gliteratti, grew unsafe and stayed that way.

Although the Shaw riot is considered to have been a popular eruption of racial outrage, it was instigated by a radical minority. The men behind the torching were Marion Barry, who was with the Student Nonviolent Coordinating Committee (SNCC) and would later become mayor, and his marxist friend Stokely Carmichael. Barry had come to Washington in the 1960s as the SNCC's first chairman. Carmichael had been active in the SNCC's work organizing against landlords in New York, and after a brief tour of Havana, Moscow, Hanoi, and Conakry, came to Washington in 1968 to help Barry fight for better housing laws. Although Barry and Carmichael often locked horns, they had a common enemy:

whites. As historian Fred Siegel puts it in *The Future Once Happened Here: New York, D.C., L.A., and the Fate of America's Big Cities*, "in the revolutionary summer of 1968 that played out against the backdrop of the American defeats in Vietnam and the previous year's rioting in Detroit and Newark, Carmichael took the role of rhetorical Trotsky to Barry's organizationally masterful Stalin."

Barry was often less volatile than Carmichael, preferring to make ambiguous pronouncements about the probability of violence, before presenting himself to guilty white liberals as the only one who could prevent it. In 1967, Barry had warned that there could be riots if Washington didn't deal with its housing problems: "Like I believe, as far as blacks are concerned, we should use all and every means we want to, and those persons who want to go out and shoot policemen, that's their thing. You know it's not mine." In other words, I don't support the violence, but really I do. In the end Barry was as responsible as Carmichael for stirring up the resentment that engulfed the city.

When Dr. King was murdered, all bets were off. "White America killed Dr. King last night," Carmichael told a crowd of young black men ready to riot. "They declared war on us. . . . There no longer needs to be discussion. Black people know when they need to get guns." In a 1988 *Washington Post* interview, Carmichael recalled: "My role would be to properly coordinate [the riot], to inflict as much damage as possible on the enemy and then to receive as much concession [as possible] from the enemy on behalf of the people."

The riot dealt Shaw a death blow, costing the city twelve hundred buildings, five thousand jobs, and almost twenty-five million dollars in damage. It was the third-costliest riot in American history, though there were only twelve deaths, all fire-related—a low number for a riot. Yet it wasn't the starving and destitute throwing bricks, but well-fed radicals in Carmichael's army. The number of Washington's black family's with incomes over eight thousand dollars had doubled in the 1960s; the number with incomes over sixteen thousand dollars had tripled. About 90 percent of the rioters had jobs, as did 80 percent of those who were arrested. As Siegel puts it, "This was a riot, befitting a city of government workers, against private property, not against people."

Washington was hostage to "riot politics." In one famous television spot, Barry soothed an agitated young brother who called the police "pigs who deserve to die." Barry, on camera, reasoned that there were other methods of action that were more acceptable. "The message was clear," Siegel writes. "Negotiate with Barry, meet his economic demands, or there would be more trouble." Siegel observes that "Many liberals were willing, even eager, given the opportunity, to surrender their old civil rights principles to a black militant willing to offer partial expiation and the promise of restraint."

Things never got better. In the 1980s, a heavy drug trade, fueled by crack, took over Shaw. A 1981 *Washington Post* article dubbed Seventh and T, once a social focus of black Washington, the city's "meanest corner." As a black barber who had worked the corner for twenty years told a reporter,

"the main problem here? People used to be more civilized."
While the Howard was rented out for an occasional go-go
show, the *Washington Post* described the scene at Seventh and
T as "a gathering place for dejected men and women, worn
thin by life." In 1986, the Howard was sold to the Washington, D. C., city government, which promptly padlocked it.

Urban flight, by blacks and whites alike, accelerated. Between 1991 and 1993, the city lost thirty thousand residents,
almost as many as in the entire 1980s. Even as the population shrank, the government grew. In 1970, there were
757,000 residents Washington, D.C., and forty thousand government employees. In 1995, there were 586,000 residents
and an estimated fifty-six thousand government workers.
Though leaders like Walter Fauntleroy, Eleanor Holmes
Norton, and Jesse Jackson repeatedly cited racism as the root
of the city's problem, what was destroying the city and sending people out to the suburbs in herds wasn't race. Larger,
psychological, cultural, and spiritual problems had infected
all urban black communities—and all of America—in the
1960s and 1970s.

∾

THE FIRST AND MOST OBVIOUS PROBLEM is what Fred Siegel
refers to in *The Future Once Happened Here* as "the moral de-
regulation of public space." After the riots, it seemed that
things that had once been unthinkable in public became
commonplace. Filthy, disheveled drug addicts and winos

slept on sidewalks, hostile panhandlers harassed pedestrians, and people no longer bothered to get dressed up when they left the house. Supreme Court decisions of the 1960s like *Coastes v. Cincinnati* and *Papachristou v. City of Jacksonville* dismantled city ordinances against loitering and vagrancy. The problem was the disintegration of what urban historian Jane Jacobs, in her 1961 classic, *The Death and Life of Great American Cities*, called "the civilized but essentially dignified and reserved terms" on which the city's public spaces operated.

The chaos in America's cities has accelerated during economic boom times. In New York City, robbery rates were stable through the twentieth century, including during the Great Depression. But robbery quintupled from 1962 to 1967, then doubled again from 1967 to 1972. At the same time, crime exploded in Washington, a city whose government employees are not dependent on heavy industry for their paychecks. These urban calamities were the fruit of a poisonous mix of radical politics, poor work habits, and an explosion of American affluence, as journalist Joe Klein pungently revealed in a 1996 article in the *New Republic*. First, noted Klein, was radical politics, which had separated liberalism from the moral foundations it had during the New Deal: "The great moral tragedy of post–New Deal liberalism was the tendency not only to absolve antisocial behavior, but also to memorialize it as a revolt against shallow and restrictive 'bourgeois' values. There was a tacit alliance between the intelligentsia and the poor, a romanticization of alienation.

Later, as the body count ballooned, this metastasized into a sloppy, undifferentiated empathy. We dare not 'blame the victim' of self-indulgence."

Klein noted that Senator Daniel Patrick Moynihan's report on the devastation caused by the disintegrating black family came out in 1965, when most urban jobs "had not yet fled." Furthermore, asked Klein, "isn't it possible that this new poverty—the chronic anarchy and dependency that began to manifest itself in the 1960s—is primarily a disease of affluence?" To the inner city poor, the "voluptuous festival of American excess [that] materialized in the living rooms of slums each night [in the 1960s]" caused jobs that once provided stability—jobs as porters, janitors, ushers—to be "suddenly derided as 'dead end,' [by those] who found it profitable to cultivate the alienation of others."

This was a long way from the days when black people of every social status were respected as long as they worked, and no one felt embarrassed by what he did for a living. As Robert McNeil, a photographer raised in Shaw, recounted in *Visual Journal*, "[in Shaw] there were black people, and they were respected black people. You had the iceman who came to the house; you had the people who handled the moving. The lawyers, the teachers; they depended on each other in a sense so that there was diversity within a neighborhood. No one resented anyone else in particular."

But perhaps most devastating were the psychological changes that came during the 1960s—particularly the rise of a new culture of narcissism, described by Christopher Lasch in his book *The Culture of Narcissism*. Citing Freudian theory, Lasch claimed that a newborn is not capable of distinguishing between itself and the world. This leads to a sense of omnipotence, which is challenged when the infant discovers that its parents not only provide gratification but frustration. This leads to different fantasies: of primal union, of the denial of dependence, and of the parents as all good or all bad. As George Scialabba put it in his examination of Lasch's work, published in 1995 in *Dissent* magazine, "According to psychoanalytic theory, the repression of infantile rage and the fantasies that result are universal and unavoidable. It is what happens thereafter that determines the degree of the child's—and the adult's—maturity or pathology. What must occur, if emotional health is to be achieved, is a gradual scaling down of the superhuman size that the parents have assumed in the infant's fantasies, and a gradual softening and displacement ('sublimation') of the intense, overwhelming feelings they have called forth."

Lasch saw several ways to achieve displacement and make a child a healthy adult. The first was discipline from the parents, which helps break down oversized fantasies. Then there is the importance of a community—those watchful eyes described at the tellabration—which helps the child escape from what Scialabba referred to as the "excessive solicitude of the contemporary over-anxious mother." Then there are "transitional objects," "playthings, games, and other objects and activities that symbolically express unconscious attachments but at the same time provide the child with reliable links to a stable, comprehensible external world."

And if displacement does not occur? "The result is a neurotic adult," Scialabba explained.

> Neurotic, Lasch asserted, in specific and predictable ways: wary of intimate, permanent relationships, which entail dependence and thus may trigger infantile rage; beset by feelings of inner emptiness and unease, and therefore ravenous for admiration and emotional and sexual conquest; preoccupied with personal "growth" and the consumption of novel sensations; prone to alternating self-images of grandiosity and abjection; liable to feel toward everyone in authority the same combination of rage and terror that the infant feels for those it depends on; unable to identify emotionally with past and future generations and therefore unable to accept the prospect of aging, decay, and death.

Here is an explanation for much of that has gone wrong in the world. In America's obsession with fitness and personal appearance, our me-first race-obsessed politics and the therapeutic culture that has taken over our public life, we have become a narcissistic people. It was also a good diagnosis of what had caused my own radicalism. I had grown up in one of the wealthiest parts of Washington, D.C., during a time of peace, in the most tolerant and free country in the history of the world, yet I had grown aggrieved and resentful towards my country. Somehow, previous generations who had nothing and had gone through hell seemed more well-adjusted. It became obvious that my problems, like those of the rest of the left, had been more personal than philosophical. They stemmed from a lack of self-discipline, from having had it too easy. My generation, like the boomers that preceded us, had been spoiled rotten and raised in a culture that exalts rebellion and lacks charm. As a result, we were mentally and spiritually weaker than our materially impoverished but steadfast grandparents. Like the president who led us, we lacked a core. Scialabba summed it up this way: "the character of selfhood has changed, from a strong (often rigid) self, in secure possession of fundamental values but riddled (often crippled) with specific anxieties, to a weak, beleaguered self, often full of charms and wiles, and capable, but only fitfully, of flights of idealism and imagination." The Narcissist, he wrote, "is currently, as Lasch claimed and clinical literature attests, the most common form of emotional pathology—the neurotic personality of our time."

As for a way out, Lasch's solutions were surprisingly uncomplicated—"localism, self-help, and community action," as well as "the homely comforts of love, work, and family life, which connect us to a world that is independent of our wishes yet responsive to our needs." But when vibrant neighborhoods like Shaw were lost, such a world disappeared. Yet in the years leading up to the tellabration at Howard, I had found a remnant of this world, of all places, on a dance floor.

TWO

To the Outskirts of Town

Gordon Parks / The Library of Congress

A drug store in Washington, D.C., 1942.
A great, good place.

ON THE MORNING OF TUESDAY, APRIL 20, 1999, Americans were confronted with a grisly and unbelievable sight. Columbine, a high school in the wealthy Colorado suburb of Littleton, was under siege. Two heavily-armed students, Eric Harris and Dylan Klebold, had entered the school and opened fire, killing thirteen people, including one teacher. Gruesome, terrifying scenes of students, some bleeding, filled homes across the country.

The reaction was immediate. Liberals blamed the easy availability of guns, while conservatives blasted the decadent popular culture of rock music, television, and video games. One television pundit even announced that America was witnessing its "cultural Chernobyl," a reference to the worst nuclear accident in history. All denounced the ultraviolent video games to which Harris and Klebold seemed to have been addicted.

There was another aspect of the tragedy on which both left and right agreed: part of the problem of Littleton was related to the problem of "place" in America. Littleton was described as the quintessential American suburb, a place of money, green lawns, peace, and social normalcy. But could it be that Littleton's modern design was exactly its problem? If the culture of narcissism had resulted from the loss of "transitional objects and communities" that help usher children into healthy adulthood, the main problem isn't only broken families, but suburbs themselves.

In recent years, journalists and social scientists of all political stripes have realized this. Along with a growing group of architects, politicians, and town planners representing a movement called the New Urbanism, they blame where we live—rather than how we live—for a host of social, psychological, and spiritual problems. The main reason so many Americans and their kids are irritable, uncultured, and solipsistic is not television or politics. We have destroyed all sense of place and life on a human scale.

In Shaw in the 1930s and 1940s you could walk down U Street and pass five theaters and tens of shops and businesses in a matter of blocks. Such a common-sense environment fostered community. As one tellebrator at Howard recalled, "everyone within five miles knew me." Lasch insisted that this kind of community is vital for psychological health.

Today, such community is gone, the victim of bad zoning and overdevelopment in the suburbs. The New Urbanist credo is most pungently spelled out by journalist James Howard Kunstler. In his books *The Geography of Nowhere* and its sequel, *Home from Nowhere*, Kunstler decries America's modern landscape—its "clogged highways, strip malls, tract house, franchise fry pits, parking lots, junked

cities and ravaged countryside"—as the source of the kind
of social ills that are "bankrupting us economically, socially,
ecologically, and spiritually."

The United States now spends almost two hundred million dollars a day on streets and roads, and the Federal Highway Administration predicts that congestion will quadruple
on freeways in the next twenty years and double on smaller
roads. This means travel delays will skyrocket to 5.6 billion
hours, costing an estimated seventy-four billion dollars a
year in lost work time. Worse is the cost in human alienation
and isolation. In the suburbs, with their lack of common
space, you can live down the street from someone for twenty
years and never meet him.

In the 1990s, suburbs even became the target of conservatives, who seemed finally to realize that people formed together in communities can fend for themselves, but that
disconnection from neighbors can often breed shameless-
ness and dependence on state agencies. Architect Andres
Duany, the man most identified with the New Urbanist movement and whose firm is developing thirty-five "new urbanist"
towns, is a critic of the suburbs, but also a defender of capitalism. "The congested, unsatisfying suburban sprawl and
disintegrating city centers of today are not the product of
laissez-faire or mindless greed," wrote Duany, whose family
fled Castro's Cuba in 1960. They are instead the "direct result
of zoning and building ordinances zealously administered by
planning departments."

In *Home from Nowhere* Kunstler argues that modern planning has actually encouraged people to become more dependent on the government by depriving them of the self-sufficiency of community living. When a kid has a noisy party, the police are called. A power outage cripples the entire town, triggering a flood of desperate calls to the power company. Dumb rules make it impossible to rent out rooms in a house. "Our affordable housing crisis is entirely of our own making," Kunstler writes. "We think the government must step in and solve this problem by going into the house-building business. In other societies ... the government gives a special tax break to anyone who puts in an accessory apartment on their property, [something that modern zoning forbids] .... We could create a vast supply of decent housing practically overnight, without bureaucracy or public funds. To make it slum proof, stipulate that it must be owner occupied. Let the landlord be the policeman."

Kunstler recalls the pre-zoning, pre-sprawl town and city planning of prewar America—places like Shaw, where there was cultural consensus about how our towns and cities should be built. Sized to human scale, rather than for automobiles, towns and cities had stores within walking distance, mixed-income living—many apartments were above shops —broad sidewalks with trees, and public transportation. The street was an orderly row of ornate façades, not the chaotic strip-mall purgatory of cheap boxy warehouses and parking lagoons. The architecture of our civic buildings, inspired by the Greeks, usually made of brick and decorated with white columns, reflected their importance. They weren't the shoe boxes of modern architecture.

∾

THIS CHANGED WITH THE RISE OF THE CAR, abetted by the single largest event in the transformation of America from a land of cities and towns to a land of suburbs: the demise of the street car. To many people, the disappearance of the trolley was simply a matter of natural selection, with poky street cars losing out to faster and more convenient automobiles. In fact, street cars were the victim of a deliberate effort by car companies and the government to monopolize the means of transportation and to subsidize highways. In 1916, the federal government subsidized cars with a seventy-five-million-dollar Federal Road Act. In 1925, highway spending was over one billion dollars. In contrast, streetcar companies got virtually no support. Then General Motors acquired the Yellow Coach company, and joining with their parts suppliers, demolished street cars and converted their routes to bus lines. Cars, combined with new technologies like the telephone and electricity, made it easier to get out of the cities. The government helped: in 1934, the Federal Housing Authority began to insure low-interest mortgages for suburban families.

After that, cars and car-related problems, began to pile up. As Kunstler notes, after World War II, new ideas about zoning and transportation were "taken to an absurd extreme. Zoning itself began to overshadow all the historic elements of civic art and civic life . . . shopping was declared an obnoxious industrial activity around which people shouldn't be allowed to live. This tended to destroy age-old physical relationships between shopping and living, as embodied, say, in Main Street." To be fair, some of these rules sprang from humane impulses. It's true that once upon a time in America people lived in tight-knit, mixed-income urban communities with dance halls, corner taverns, and a local church. But during the Industrial Revolution there were also people living dangerously close to factories. Americans, frightened by the infiltration of residential areas by polluting industries, came up with rules to separate industries from homes, a logical measure. Moreover, cities have always been far from perfect. Dirt, disease, and crime have always been features of the metropolis. Classic blues songs like "Ain't Nobody's Business" and "I'm Gonna Move to the Outskirts of Town" expressed the claustrophobia of urban living and the desire to break away. The roots of the modern suburb go back to the 1920s when developers first began to lure wealthy city dwellers to the country with the idea of having their own "manor." Nevertheless, the automobile was at the time still a new invention, and the threat of mass exodus remote.

Suburbs were also, in many ways, nice places to live. To many of the people who moved there, the suburbs could be a small slice of heaven. To the generation that was exhausted from fighting the war, the suburbs offered green space to breathe and raise children free of the problems of the city. Even today, I can appreciate the psychology of relief the suburbs can offer, the idea of putting some space, a buffer of peace and quiet, between you and the workplace. But like the cultural revolutions of the 1960s, which sought to correct perceived problems of the 1950s, suburban planners went too far. They became ubiquitous, and went a little mad with power.

In October of 1997, PBS aired "Divided Highways," a documentary about the history of America's highway system. As critics in the film noted, the highway system was the largest, most intrusive big government project in the history of humanity, and its creation of our placeless culture had nothing to do with the inexorable currents of the free market. Do conservatives want to talk about arrogant, power-crazed Washington meddling? How about the tens of thousands of homes in Seattle, Miami, Philadelphia, and other cities and towns unceremoniously razed by the federal government to make room for giant overpasses filled with so much fast-moving traffic that conducting business in the neighborhood, much less walking down the street in peace, was impossible? These often safe, self-sufficient, and vibrant black communities were bulldozed because they occupied the cheapest land available and because at the time the residents had no political power. When it came to the behemoth highway system, one person noted in "Divided Highways," "the government just did whatever it wanted." The government never built as much housing as it destroyed. It even wanted to build a highway along Fisherman's Wharf in San Francisco, but was rebuffed by the mayor. "There was a kind of fanaticism in the highway lobby," recalls then–San Francisco Mayor Joseph Alioto. "Had anybody suggested that we might save a block or two on the way to the Sistine Chapel, they'd have built a highway right through the Vatican."

Probably the most tragic story told on "Divided Highways," and the most representative, was that of Overtown, in Miami. For most of its history, Overtown was, as one resident remembered, "the hub of black business, black civic life, black professional life, black entertainment. . . . street life was exciting and dynamic. The restaurants were full of people." In the early 1960s, the federal government put a stretch of the interstate highway system through the heart of this Florida version of Shaw, effectively killing what was an active, business-friendly town. It had been a town that was a place, but by 1968 thirty thousand of the forty thousand residents had moved or been driven out by the construction. Now, like much of urban America, it looks like the surface of Mars.

Overtown's fate as the victim of what one historian calls "a political drive-by shooting" was all too representative of what was going on all over the country. Soon America was a place not of corner taverns, dance halls, and lively streets, but of strip malls, beltways, traffic jams, and the alienation of neighbors and generations.

∽

EVEN WHEN THE EARLY SUBURBS were first going up, people sensed there was something deeply flawed about them. The left lambasted the phoniness of middle-class living space. In the 1950s they condemned what one critic called "the crabgrass frontier" of postwar America. Levittown, the original suburb, was denounced as the ultimate in bourgeois conformity. Architect Lewis Mumford described it as "a multitude of uniform, unidentifiable houses, lined up inflexibly, at uniform distances on uniform roads, in a treeless command waste, inhabited by people of the same class, the same incomes, the same age group, witnessing the same television performances, eating the same tasteless prefabricated foods, from the same freezers, conforming in every outward and inward to a common mold manufactured in the same central metropolis." Mumford concluded that "the ultimate effect of the suburban escape in our time is, ironically, a low-grade uniform environment from which escape is impossible." He was joined by the critic Ron Rosenbaum, who announced that the film *The Invasion of the Body Snatchers* was "about the horror of being in the 'burbs. About neighbors whose lives had so lost their individual distinctness they could be taken over by alien vegetable pods—and no one would know the difference."

This critique persists, but now conservatives are the critics. The November-December 1996 issue of *The American*

Enterprise was dedicated to the New Urbanist movement. Editor Karl Zinsmeister offered "A Conservative Case Against Suburbia," and he cast his net wide: "The hurried life, the disappearance of family time, the weakening of generational links, our ignorance of history, our lack of local ties, an exaggerated focus on money, the anonymity of community life, the rise of radical feminism, the decline of civic action, the tyrannical dominance of television and pop culture over leisure time—all of these problems have been fed, and in some cases instigated, by suburbanization, in ways that few people anticipated a generation ago when mass suburbs were first created."

Zinsmeister claimed that Betty Friedan's 1963 ur-feminist work, *The Feminist Mystique*, was an "anguished cry" from suburban Westchester County, a plea for a sense of place where there was none. "Americans who would prefer that their wives and daughters not follow Friedan down the path to NOW-style feminism," Zinsmeister warned, "would do well to think hard about how the current structure of our suburban communities feeds this problem." He cited authorities like Kunstler and Jane Jacobs, who was the first to note that well-designed communities, even if inhabited by the poor, have a thriving social life and a natural crime deterrent in people who populate pedestrian-friendly streets.

Zinsmeister also put a stake in the heart of the claim, popular among many conservatives, that suburbanization is simply the result of the natural flow of the free market. The government, after all, offered incentives for new families to move to the suburbs in the form of low-interest mortgages and billions in road-building programs. Such moves guaranteed, as Zinsmeister noted, that "new thoroughfares . . . wrecked many existing communities, city neighborhoods were slashed by elevated highways, and outlying towns had the life snuffed out of them by beltways and controlled-access interstates."

Perhaps most disastrous, suburbs further served to separate children from their fathers. According to Christopher Lasch, one of the main culprits in creating a narcissistic personality is the absence of a father. Without daily contact with and discipline from a father, children have trouble breaking down and civilizing the overgrown fantasies they experience as infants. Lasch describes one case in which a girl's father and uncle both died when she was very young. The woman "wavered between her feelings of grandiosity and an awareness that she was not as grandiose as she wanted to be." Because her mother refused to remarry and "showered the child with attentions," she—the mother—"made it clear that the child was to substitute for the dead father and uncle." The result was a narcissistic, neurotic woman with "feelings of unworthiness and violent oscillations of self-esteem. . . . The father's death, combined with the mother's use of the child as a substitute for the father, allowed the girl's fantasy of a grandiose, phallic father to flourish without the correcting influence of everyday contact."

After the industrial revolution, most men were required to work outside the home, and the distance from their work to their suburban homes lengthened their absence. Combined with liberal bureaucracy, this absence has had a disastrous effect: "Capitalism has severed the ties of personal dependence only to revive dependence under cover of bureaucratic rationality," wrote Lasch. "Having overthrown feudalism and slavery and then outgrown its own personal and familial form, capitalism has evolved a new political ideology, welfare liberalism, which absolves individuals of moral responsibility and treats them as victims of social circumstance." The old order of "priestly and monarchial hegemony" has given way to "the managerial and professional classes which operate the corporate state." In New Deal, then suburban, America, "a new ruling class of administrators, bureaucrats, technicians, and experts has appeared, which retains so few of the attributes formerly associated with a ruling class—pride of place, the 'habit of command,' disdain for the lower orders—that its existence as a class often goes unnoticed." The "propertied elite" has been driven to the margins, replaced by "the new therapeutic culture of narcissism."

Today, Levittown seems like a communal utopia compared to places like Littleton, where the seamless web of community and culture that had sustained people like the residents of Shaw prior to the 1960s is completely gone. "Those mothers aren't on the front porches anymore," William Bennett told a reporter for NBC news at the time of the shooting. "We've become reluctant to step in and scold other people's children." Bennett noted that Littleton's two murderers had a long history of trouble, had flirted with Nazism, and stalked around school in black trench coats. "The question of Columbine," said Bennett, "is, 'If you saw a couple kids walking down the street in black trench coats and saluting Hitler, would you do anything?'"

Probably not. A few weeks after the Littleton massacre, Lakis Polycarpou, a former student at Columbine High School, wrote a piece for the *Washington Post* about his home town. It wasn't the tight community depicted in the media coverage following the massacre:

> In the aftermath of last month's shooting, there has been much talk about how it has devastated "the community" and how "the community" would pull together. While true, it also sounds strange to me, as I always pictured community as something that happened anywhere but a place like the Littleton area. We never knew our neighbors, except in passing; we certainly never had any social connection to them. Children rarely played outside on the street, as I had in elementary school [in a different town]. As far as I knew, no one in my family ever joined a "neighborhood community". . . . There was no pool, no ice rink, no town square in the area around Columbine. Neighbors moved into homes and then moved out, and it was often some time before you realized the people next door were new.

Polycarpou then offers this grim conclusion: "Against the backdrop of this interchangeable world, with minimal connection to others, it's not difficult to imagine a student so dissociated from his environment and himself that prefabricated, reductive fantasy replaces reality."

In other words, the narcissistic fantasies that Lasch recognized could only be dispelled by community and adult intervention had exploded partially because of a lack of place. This was pointed out by Christopher Caldwell in the pages of the conservative magazine *National Review* shortly after the shootings. Caldwell noted that the suburbs of the 1950s and 1960s were often built as adjuncts to established cities like New York and Washington. Such places boasted village greens and, in many cases, sidewalks and nearby towns. Caldwell described the "eastern suburb" where he was raised as providing "gradual and supervised. . . . entry into adult mobility." A five-year-old could walk around the neighborhood, a ten-year-old "all over town," and fourteen-year-olds could ride their bikes to other towns."

Compared to this, wrote Caldwell, the sprawling western suburbs of the late twentieth century are like prisons:

> The problem in affluent "McMansion" suburbs like Littleton is that children grow up in almost hermetic seclusion—a newer and more soul-destroying condition, with dismal implications for democracy. Large lots, dead-end streets, and draconian zoning laws mean that there are vast distances to travel to reach any kind of

public space. . . . Critics of the Fifties complained that Levittown's sameness could lead to conformity—although there was never much proof that it did. Today's critics warn that the loneliness of Littleton produces something very like the opposite of conformity. We can only hope that the evidence they're right doesn't continue to mount.

~

LIKE CALDWELL, I grew up in an eastern suburb—Potomac, outside of Washington, D.C. Like Littleton, Potomac suffers from car dependence, lack of personal contact, and mind-crushing boredom for pre-driving teens. However, Potomac has what suburbs in Colorado and Arizona lack: a culturally exciting, centralized urban playground, easily accessible by public transportation. After graduating from high school, I enrolled at the Catholic University of America in the Northeast part of D.C., not far from Capitol Hill and Shaw. I had no car, but there is a subway stop on campus. The subway line runs from the school through the heart of Washington and then out to the suburbs, stopping not far from my parents' house.

I never missed having a car. The subway could get me to any bar, restaurant, museum, or office in Washington—or in suburban Maryland and Virginia. It didn't take long before I was seeing some of the same faces over and over again, including the people I had known in high school, because we weren't scattered for miles around as we would have been in Littleton. We formed bonds of friendship and community that lasted. We became "regulars" at certain bars and would often bump into each other at unexpected moments. It wasn't uncommon to take a date to a movie, drinks, then a late-night bite to eat and cross paths with half a dozen friends you hadn't expected to see. One night after I got off work very late (I was working in a movie theater) I stopped at a nearby diner. Sitting in three different booths were people I knew from high school and college, as well as an actor who had been in a show with my brother. Even encountering friends from grade school was fairly common.

In short, Washington is, like other great cities, a place of third places. In his book *The Great Good Place: Cafes, Coffee Shops, Community Centers, Beauty Parlors, General Stores, Bars, Hangouts and How They Get You Through the Day*, sociologist Ray Oldenburg describes the problem he thinks is eating away at the soul of America: the death of the "third place." According to Oldenburg, third places are those spots—the bars, coffee shops, and cafes mentioned in the title—that provide a healthy social environment away from home and work. He notes that third places "exist on neutral ground and serve to level their guests to a condition of social equality." Young and old interact according to unwritten laws of civility. Conversation is the main activity, with the place's character "determined most of all by its regular clientele and marked by a playful mood" and a certain "spiritual tonic" often fostered by dim lighting and alcohol. They are also places where—and this is crucial—people can do nothing.

Perhaps the third place's greatest attribute is its ability to foster basic human decency. According to Oldenburg, in third places "whatever hint of hierarchy exists is predicated upon human decency" rather than wealth or fame, and a kind of natural restraint holds sway. Boisterous or political talk is welcome, but not someone who brags or hogs the floor. Young and old interact, making it difficult for the young to speak and act the way they might at a keg party or in a rock club. As Oldenburg notes, this decency often spills into the larger community: "Promotion of decency in the third place is not limited to it. The regulars are not likely to do any of those things roundly disapproved at the coffee counter."

As an example of a town that had real third places, Oldenburg examines life in 1940 in River Park, a small town in Minnesota not unlike Bedford Falls in *It's a Wonderful Life*. Lacking television or easy travel, the citizens relied on each other: "In talking with one another and in appreciating one another's antics, escapades, accomplishments, and misfortunes, people's days were made interesting." This was only possible, writes Oldenburg, because "of the forty commercial establishments along Main Street," nineteen regularly encouraged hanging around and visiting. One of these was Bertram's Drug Store. There, one could find the front steps "festooned with boys," kids playing cribbage or other games in the booths opposite the soda fountain, and old men in the back playing poker. The line of seats in front of the soda fountain itself was "only rarely unoccupied."

But Bertram's was only the beginning. River Park—a place without a pool hall, movie theater, or bowling alley—had no fewer than three barber shops and five "3.2 joints," cafe-type buildings that served beer and food and provided a juke box. It was in these places that the young were ushered into the adult world. It also had a lively post office where towns-folk had to go to get their mail (there was no delivery.) People were constantly in the streets, bringing themselves into daily contact with their fellow citizens. Oldenburg notes that in River Park, practical jokes—which are unheard of and would probably lead to lawsuits in a modern suburb—were common. "The practical joke comes into its own only when its victim is well and widely known, where people are intensely interested in one another, and where social ties between people are not fragile."

Yet in encouraging people to do nothing, third places allow them to do no less than keep democracy alive. In *The Revolt of the Elites*, Christopher Lasch took up Oldenburg's cry, noting how third places "historically . . . have been the natural haunts of pamphleteers, agitators, politicos, newspapermen, revolutionaries, and other verbal types." He connected the disappearance of third places and the death of civic life—and ultimately democracy itself. As neighborhood hangouts give way to suburban shopping malls, or on the other hand, to private cocktail parties, the essentially political art of conversation is replaced by shoptalk or personal gossip. Increasingly, said Lasch, "conversation literally has no place in American society."

Duke Ellington came of age in a third place: Frank Holliday's poolroom next to the Howard Theater. "It was the high spot for billiard parlors," Ellington recalled, "where all the kids from all neighborhoods came, and the great pool sharks from all over town. Some would come from out of town, too, and there would be championship matches. Guys from all walks of life seemed to converge there: school kids over and under sixteen; college students and graduates, some starting out in law and medicine and science; and lots of Pullman porters and dining-car waiters." Also present were piano players, both conservatory trained and self-taught. But the best thing about the poolroom, recalled Ellington, "was the *talk*. Frank Holliday's poolroom sounded as if the prime authorities on *every* subject had been assembled there. Baseball, football, basketball, boxing, wrestling, racing, medicine, law, politics—everything was discussed with authority. Frank Holliday's poolroom was a great place."

Not exactly the modern teenage world of video games and MTV, but Ellington seemed to get by. His fondness for Holliday's reveals how the death of the third place is as serious a sociological problem as crime, drugs, welfare, or anything else. As Lasch put it, in the last forty years we have created a world lacking "urban amenities, conviviality, conversation, politics—almost everything, in short, that makes life worth living."

Ironically, even as Littleton was dismantling the idea of the suburb as a pristine and crime-free enclave, one troubled city was growing safer by changing its structure. Just days after Littleton, the *Washington Post* reported a dramatic change that had taken place in the Baltimore community of Pleasant View—once a slum, seething with crime, drugs, and nondescript highrises. These buildings had been based on designs by modernist European architects, who believe that buildings should simply be utilitarian boxes. The result was an ugly, dispiriting landscape that bred disorder and hopelessness. "It gives you a feeling of despair," one woman said. "You're locked up in a cage with a fence around you and everything stinks."

The government decided to tear down the Pleasant View highrises and try again, replacing them with low-rise and low-density apartment buildings. Vacant lots were made into recreation centers. The result? A precipitous drop in crime. "The only sound was the murmur of the jungle gym at sunset," reported the *Post*. "Police officers chatted with residents on the sidewalk. Street corners [where drug dealers once prowled] were empty."

It seemed as if inner-city and suburban residents were switching places. Cities were becoming more safe and communal, while suburbs were collapsing. Suburban kids would be trapped in a world without community, fun, adventure, romance. Stuck in a placeless place, they would be left to soak up the sewage coming through cable, on records, and in video games.

There would have been no hope at all if a cultural counterrevolution hadn't taken place in April 1998.

THREE

Blast from the Past

The Library of Congress, Theodor Horydczak Collection

Glen Echo's Spanish Ballroom, circa 1940.

O N APRIL 21, 1998, forty million Americans tuned in for the season finale of *ER*, one of the most popular shows in the history of television. Yet the most remarkable thing about that night's episode was a commercial for Gap clothing, which ran about midway through the show. Against a snow-white backdrop, to the jumping sounds of Louis Prima's 1956 swing song "Jump, Jive & Wail," a group of young people danced the lindy hop, the swing dance that had reigned in America from the 1920s to the 1950s.

The effect was electric, instant, and pervasive. Literally overnight, swing dancing once again became part of American popular culture. It was the first time swing had been seen on such a scale since the 1940s. The commercial had introduced an entire generation—two entire generations—to the tight, stylish turns of lindy hop. The next day, telephones at dance studios began ringing off the hook with calls, many from teenagers, about "that Gap dance." Within weeks, ballrooms and dance classes filled, albums by neo-swing groups became bestsellers, and swing was the topic of a media blitz that included articles in *Entertainment Weekly*, the *Wall Street Journal*, the *New York Times*, and *Rolling Stone*. There were television spots on swing on CNN, CBS, the *The News Hour with Jim Lehrer*, and VH1.

In a way, the swing tsunami wasn't completely unexpected. In 1996, an independent film called *Swingers* had been released. The film depicts the lives of young actors in Los Angeles and features swing dancing, which was enjoying a small underground rebirth in Los Angeles at the time. The film was a surprise hit, attracting the interest of the media as well as Madison Avenue. The renewed interest in swing dancing that follwed swept the country after the Gap ad aired: it reached an audience more than ten times the size of *Swingers'*.

~

THERE WERE A FEW PEOPLE who had been swinging before *Swingers*. I started swing dancing in 1995, when I was thirty-one, not long after I discovered Christopher Lasch. I had given up drinking, my liberalism was cracking, and I was looking for something fun to do apart from Washington's bar scene. I remembered that there was a place near my house that featured swing on Saturday nights, an old building called the Spanish Ballroom that had been built in the late 1920s as part of Glen Echo amusement park. The park had shut down in the late 1960s, but the ballroom was still functional. It had been a bandstand for the Dorsey brothers, Benny Goodman, and other swing greats.

It is also considered by many to be a sacred place. The ballroom is the size of a small airplane hangar, and although there is no heat or air conditioning, it has a dusty, antiquated charm. A line of windows overlooking the Potomac river lets in shafts of warm yellow light in the afternoons. The ceiling is pockmarked with holes from water damage and fallen tiles, and the paint on the bandstand is peeling, but this only adds to the ambiance. The energy of the generations of dancers who have stomped there remains palpable. For someone raised in a suburb, it is antiquity itself.

Then there's the floor. Blond maple and "pond smooth," as one writer called it, it is the original floor laid in 1933. Considered one of the best in the nation, its spring is soft on knees and attracts dancers from hundreds of miles away. This is a place where our parents and grandparents jitter-bugged, waltzed, and fell in love. It is a reprieve from the paving and malling of America, a link to the past in a culture obsessed with the present.

When I arrived at my first dance in the winter of 1995, I entered another world. The eighteen-piece Tom Cunningham Orchestra, the most popular big band in Washington, was blasting out "Shorty George," a song originally made famous by Count Basie. It was a giddy, ringing sound, a dose of aural prozac for someone raised on the grim self-importance of rock music. There were hundreds of people from end to end of the great hall lindy-hopping like mad.

While there are conflicting accounts, many people believe that the lindy hop began on June 17, 1928, with a dancer named George "Shorty" Snowden, during a dance marathon held at the Manhattan Casino. The ballroom was packed to the walls for the nonsegregated event; both Walter Winchell and Ed Sullivan attended, both covering the event for the *New York Graphic*. Shorty Snowden, who was known as one of the best dancers in New York, grew tired of doing the same fox trot with his partner. He suddenly executed a "breakaway," gracefully separating from his partner for a few seconds and doing some solo steps. The crowd, which was woozy from watching days of dancing, came to life. Someone asked Snowden what he was doing. "The lindy," he replied—referring to Charles Lindberg's recent "hop" across the Atlantic—and a new dance was born. (The New York health department shut down the marathon on the Fourth of July, forcing Snowden to share the five thousand dollar prize with three other couples.)

Snowden was one of the prime attractions at the Savoy Ballroom in Harlem, which at the time of the dance marathon was only two years old but already world famous. Although largely forgotten, for a little over thirty years the Savoy, "the home of happy feet," was one of America's great third places and most impressive cultural institutions. According to historian David Levering Lewis in his book *When Harlem Was in Vogue*, "the March 12, 1926 opening of the Savoy shook America as profoundly in its own way as the 1913 Armory Show [which introduced modern art to America] had turned the world of mainstream art inside out. Archi- tecturally, the Savoy dazzled with a spacious lobby framing a huge, cut-glass chandelier and marble staircase, an orange and blue dance hall with soda fountain, tables, and heavy carpeting covering half its area, the remainder a burnished dance floor, 250 by fifty feet, with two bandstands and a dis- appearing stage at the end." The Savoy took up an entire city block, from 140th to 141st street. It was also integrated and could hold five thousand people. Classical composers like Stravinsky and Poulenc came there to listen to Chick Webb (with a young Ella Fitzgerald on vocals), Count Basie, and Benny Goodman. According to artist Romare Bearden, "The best dancing in the world was there, and the best music." If you wanted to be where culture was happening, claimed Bearden, "You'd either want to be in Harlem or in Paris."

Lindy spread across the country and into mainstream society in the thousands of ballrooms that sprang up during the swing era (1935-1945). The dance became diluted by less skilled imitators, becoming East Coast swing and eventually dying out. Music historians looking for the causes of its death point to the material shortages of World War II—which made it hard to produce records and raised the expense of hiring a full big band—as well as the rise of rock and bebop jazz, a style better suited for listening than for dancing. Yet an often overlooked development might be the most impor- tant: taxes. In 1944, a 30-percent federal excise tax was lev- ied against night clubs that had dancing. Jazz great Max

Roach recalled the devastating effect the tax had on dancing and other entertainment: "It was levied on all places where they had entertainment. It was levied in case they had public dancing, signing, storytelling, humor, or jokes on stage. This tax is the real story behind why dancing, not just tap dancing, but public dancing per se and also singing, quartets, comedy, all these kinds of thing, were just out."

But when I stepped into the Spanish Ballroom for the first time in 1995, it was as though the last sixty years of American history had never happened. I shuffled hesitantly towards the stage and was about to sit down when a woman about my mother's age asked me to dance.

"I don't know how," I stammered.

"I'll show you." She grabbed my wrist and pulled me out on the floor.

We stood in the middle of the floor. She took my left hand in her right, then told me to put my hand on her back.

"Can you count to six?" she said.

"Sure."

"Okay, step to the left and hold it for a beat."

I stepped, the woman mirroring my move.

"Now do the same thing to the right."

I stepped to the right and held.

"Now step back and forward with your left foot."

I stepped.

"Now put all three together."

I stepped left, then right, then back.

"You're doing it!" she cried.

I was. I was dancing. I felt a rush of exhilaration, like the feeling when your dad releases you on your bike for the first time.

At that moment, pandemonium erupted in the ballroom. A drum began pounding out a solo that seemed familiar to everyone in the place but me, and people formed a gigantic circle on the floor. Then, two dancers strutted out of the circle and into the middle of the floor. The man, in his late thirties, wore a black pin-striped zoot suit, a watch chain, and two-tone wingtips. The woman, about the same age, had on a 1940s vintage pink dress. As the crowd clapped in time and the sound of the band's horn section rose from the stage— the song was "Sing, Sing, Sing," which had originally been performed by Benny Goodman—the man and woman began to dance.

It was unlike any dancing I had ever seen. The couple moved like two panthers, turning and sliding around each other. They did kicks, flawlessly mirroring one another, then he flipped her over his shoulder. She landed with a smile and a wink, held one perfect beat, and they were off again. Their performance was seamless and looked effortless. It was enchanting, a divine prayer of physical self-assurance and grace. When they finished, the roar of applause seemed to lift the ballroom off its foundation.

The dancers were Tom Koerner and Debra Sternberg, championship dancers and the heart of Washington's swing scene. They had both been jitterbugging for years before *Swingers*. Koerner first discovered swing as an undergraduate at the University of Virginia during the disco nights of the mid-1970s. "It was 1976, and the sexual revolution was going to pass me," he remembers. "I had a bad haircut, bad glasses, bad muscle tone, and hormones surging as only a Catholic's can." Koerner met some girls in his dorm who taught him shag, a kind of quick-step swing, and brought him to a dance marathon. A group of senior citizens showed up at the dance and began to dance the jitterbug, a dance considerably more complex than shag. "We made them stop what they were doing and do all their routines from the beginning," Koerner recounts. "From that moment on, I was like the guy in *Close Encounters of the Third Kind* who gets this image stuck in his head."

Koerner spent the next ten years learning lindy, watching old movies featuring dance greats like Frankie Manning and Jean Veroz, and going to law school. In 1987, he met Sternberg at the Kennedy Warren Ballroom in Washington, where the swing band Doc Scantlin and the Imperial Palms Orchestra played on Friday nights. Sternberg had taken a job as a cigarette girl at the ballroom's big band retro dance. "I was already very much into the culture of the 1930s and 1940s," she recalls, "although I didn't dance. I was shocked to discover all these people swing dancing—I had no idea this was out there! I'm the youngest of a family that was crazy about dancing, and my two sisters were avid jitterbuggers in their school days, but I am of an age where people didn't touch-dance any more. So I saw people holding hands while they danced, and I was mesmerized."

Koerner and Sternberg began dancing together, and were soon getting paid to perform—something unheard of for swing dancers in the 1980s, Sternberg points out. Then their awards began stacking up: 1994, 1995, and 1996 Virginian Lindy Hop champions and 1994 United Kingdom Lindy Hop champions. For them, swing has become something of a religion. "The music is wonderful," Sternberg says. "It's great exercise; it's a wonderful social event. People meet, form friendships, get married. Young mix with old. The geekiest find they have a talent they never knew about and have a chance to be the cool kids for a change. I see people go from being shy and insecure to being lively and ebullient."

As Koerner puts it, swing is about "America finding it's center again" after thirty years of power chords and pot smoke. "A lot of these kids learning swing don't know a thing about civility and social graces," Koerner says. "They can be from the best families in Washington, yet be totally clueless about how to behave."

∿

IN THE WAKE OF THE GAP AD, swing began achieving the miraculous: rejuvenating the third place in America.

Ballrooms had once been some of the glorious civic and social spots in America. Ralph Ellison, author of *Invisible Man*, referred to the Savoy "as one of the great centers of culture in the United states, even though it was . . . thought of as simply a place of entertainment."

In her autobiography, *Swingin' at the Savoy*, dancer Norma Miller recalls her experiences as a poor black girl in the 1930s growing up in a house behind the great ballroom. During the summer she and her sister Dot would spend their evenings on the fire escape, listening to the bands: "We were often rocked to sleep by a swinging lullaby."

In one magical passage, Miller describes her first venture into the Savoy. She was just starting junior high, and it was Easter Sunday in Harlem. A dancer nicknamed "Twist Mouth" saw her dancing on the sidewalk in front of the ballroom and asked her if she wanted to dance with him:

> I waited on the same spot, not daring to leave for fear of missing him when he came to get me. At last I saw him come back out of the doors. He came to me and took my hand. I had to run to keep up with him, we took the steps two at a time. I was breathless when I walked into the ballroom. He was moving so fast, and I was trying to take it all in. It was the most beautiful place I had ever seen. The soft lights, the music coming over the whole place, and everywhere I looked there were people dancing close together, holding hands, or walking together. I had stepped into a romantic paradise. . . . As we did our first swing-out, it seemed that Twist Mouth just lifted me in the air. My feet felt like they never touched the floor. People roared and at the end we did a step called a flying jig walk. The house

came down. At the finish, Twist Mouth hoisted me onto his shoulders and paraded me around the floor. . . . He carried me all the way to the door, put me down, and thanked me. Then he bussed me on the cheek and led me out of the ballroom. I was as happy as a kid could be. I danced all the way home.

In 1958, the Savoy was demolished and replaced by a government housing project. As much as the Kennedy assassination, Vietnam, or Watergate, the demolition of the Savoy was the death knell for a certain America, the place of self-made communities, people who knew how to dress, true entertainment, and tough spiritual resolve. When the Savoy went down, a new America emerged from the rubble. Out went style, to be replaced by drugs, rock 'n' roll (which in the beginning was just swing music played leaner and tighter), and television.

But with the return of swing, third places began struggling to make a comeback. In February 1997 Tom Koerner brought swing to a restaurant called America. Located on the ground floor of the Tyson's Corner mall, it is at the epicenter of what antisuburban activists like to call a "crudscape." Far from small town charm and city excitement, surrounded by gas stations, soulless highrises, and the Beltway, America —although boasting a comfortable atmosphere of candles, white table cloths, and high ceilings—is stuck in the gut of a mall, that quintessential American placeless place. Often when the mall shut down, so did business.

Then swing arrived. In a little over a year, the amazing occurred: America became a place. Show up on a Friday night and you'll be greeted not with Muzak, a bored hostess, and a room half-filled with people picking at their food, but the blasting horns of the Tom Cunningham Orchestra. The patrons, many of them teenagers, will be practicing moves in the isles, kidding each other, and asking adults for pointers. America is no longer an ersatz place, a mall where zombies shuffle along eye-scanning the merchandise. It's what Ray Oldenburg calls "a great good place," a spot where people of all ages and classes talk to each other and laugh, a place where people sweat and flirt, a place with sartorial style and atmosphere and memories, a place with character. "What we're seeing is the revival of the adult playground," Koerner told me between songs there one night. "People want a place where they can go that's classy and where they can unwind and not choke on smoke or hang out with grungy people."

Perhaps more than other third places, the dance hall has unwritten rules of etiquette, especially between the sexes. "It's a place to be, a place to belong," says Debra Sternberg. "It's something that single women can do by themselves and not feel awkward or on display, something that guys who're looking to meet ladies do that's not like going to the meat market. It offers all the advantages of any group activity, from belong to the ski club to going to a church social group. All this in an environment that's not based on drinking, smoking, and having sex. Just plain, good, clean fun."

At America, if you ask a women to dance and she says no, it is inappropriate to pursue the matter any further. At swing dances, men learn how to behave, something they forgot in the 1960s. In "Swing, Bop, and Hand Dancing," a documentary about the history of swing and hand dancing, a modern offshoot of swing done primarily in black communities, Rutgers ethnomusicologist Katrina Hazard-Donald sums it up nicely. "The benefits of swing go far beyond just learning cool moves," she says. "In the old days of swing, there were entire rituals surrounding the dance. Men were leaders in their community. They went and picked up their dates, then escorted them to the dance. They displayed that by being leaders on the dance floor. They learned how to ask a girl to dance, lead her onto the dance floor, then, at the end of the song, return her from where she had come."

One trip to Glen Echo or America could teach a lesson that was lost during the sexual revolution: there can be degrees of contact between the sexes. The dictum of all-or-nothing fostered by thirty years of pornography is a lie; worse, it is one that paradoxically cheats us of some of the finer sensual pleasures of human relationships. As one dance studio owner told a reporter for the *Wall Street Journal*, "Touching is nice. Socially acceptable touching promotes civilizing behavior."

The way kids have taken to swing has made it clear that those supposedly snarling, cynical, sexually and morally libertine Gen X'ers are not opposed to a little class and style.

People have always assumed that, like the baby-boomers, we have rejected the social and cultural mores of America's past. The truth is we were never offered the choice.

~

IRONICALLY, AS THE YOUTH OF AMERICA were rediscovering rules, romance, and gender, the president of the United States was debasing the culture. In January 1998 it was revealed that President Clinton had carried on an affair with a twenty-one-year-old intern named Monica Lewinsky. In fact, it hadn't been an affair, but an abusive, one-sided sexual manipulation of a subordinate by her superior.

This scandal may at first seem to have nothing to do with the swing renaissance, but there is a profound connection between the two. Clinton tried to pass Lewinsky off as a stalker, and his treatment of her highlighted the difference between his generation and the gallantry of swing dancers of the World War II era. In the 1940s, a white woman who was dating a black jazz musician went to a club to see him play. When she arrived she found herself the target of racial slurs by the other black musicians. At that point Billie Holiday appeared and told them to lay off. "But she ain't black," one of them said. "So what," Holiday shot back, "Woman is the nigger of the world." Holiday's cutting observation finds a parallel in the Lewinsky affair. While those on all sides of the scandal were obsessed with surface questions, they missed the real, obvious meaning of the affair: Bill Clinton's behavior reveals the hypocrisy and misogyny of modern liberalism and its feminist allies.

To understand how, it's necessary to turn to the pages of *Domestic Tranquility: A Brief Against Feminism*, a devastating book by Carolyn Graglia, a Justice Department lawyer who became a housewife and mother. Graglia traces modern liberalism's distrust of the feminine to the 1940s and the hysteria over "momism." Led by Philip Wylie, the critique of momism asserted that the American idolatry of femininity and the housewife was turning American males into soft and squishy drones, laboring endlessly in boring jobs just to keep the better half content. In his 1942 screed *Generation of Vipers*, Wylie railed against the "nonsensical notion of honoring and rewarding women for nothing more than being female." To support a "huge class of idle, middle aged women," he wrote, "brave and dreaming men . . . . take a stockroom job in the hairpin factory." This is a far cry from the exaltation of women by swing dancers like Frankie Manning, the octogenarian dancer and former Savoy great who still tells men, "Fella, the woman you are dancing with is a queen."

Wylie's antimomism, suggests Graglia, found its most powerful expression in 1951, when the first issue of *Playboy* hit the stands with Marilyn Monroe on the cover. "[Monroe] was everything both male rebels and feminists expected of the new woman, liberated at last from what feminists de-

picted as the stifling cocoon spun by the oppressive patriar-
chy," Graglia writes.

> Liberated Monroe surely was. Pursuing a successful ca-
> reer until she died a suicide at age thirty-six, she de-
> pended on no breadwinner. Not requiring the sexual
> revolution to unfetter her from any vestiges of con-
> stricting morality, she was the paradigmatic sexually
> liberated woman. Diana Trilling described her as
> sleeping her way to her early opportunities, and, once
> famous, continuing to be "compliant" in numberless
> sexual encounters with men and "on occasion" another
> woman. Finally, she was no mom for, to her great sad-
> ness, Monroe was unable to give birth . . . this failure,
> one might speculate, could have been related to the fact
> that she had a dozen or more abortions.

Here was the emerging modern woman embraced by
"progressives": not beholden to any one man, sexually "liberated" (which pleased countercultural leftists and sexual
predators like the beatniks and the hippies that followed
them), childless, amoral, career-driven. In other words, the
antithesis of everything that women had been, by nature it
seemed, for centuries. This kind of antifeminine animus was
also a large factor in the feminist movement, which was getting its start in the early 1960s, just as partner dancing, with
its male leader, was dying. Pioneering feminist leader Betty
Friedan referred to stay-at-home moms as "parasites," and

her followers attacked the feminine ideals of motherhood and sexual restraint. As Graglia notes, feminists "promoted a sexual revolution that encouraged women to mimic male sexual promiscuity."

As women became ever more liberated in the 1960s and 1970s, men, particularly progressive types like the future President Clinton, respected them less. Social mores began to crumble; partner dancing and its attendant respect were lost. The twist and other forms of androgynous wiggling feminized men and deprived them of a civilized way to hold and woo women. The paradox was that men, by rejecting their traditional role as the hang-up of an older generation, freed themselves of the responsibility to act like gentlemen— a problem that has only got worse, as anyone who has watched MTV knows. In the various accounts of the male New Left demonstrators of the 1960s, many men admit they attended rallies just to meet girls. Leftist women only seemed to make matters worse for themselves. A famous antidraft poster of the era depicted Joan Baez and two other women sitting over a sign announcing that "women say yes to boys who say no." As the language of sex became less lyrical, the idea that sex was meant to be mysterious and spiritual and romantic—and that there is a purpose to social con-straints—was rooted out of our culture. While the calls for equality were in some measure justified and overdue, too often the equality came at the price of denying that men and women had real differences in nature.

Feminists and their liberal male flunkies demanded equality and rejected paternalism, believing that new mores would usher in a bright era of intimacy between the sexes. What they were too myopic to see was that without the constraints of chivalry and gallantry that saddled men with the responsibility for acting like gentlemen, the sexes lost a system that allowed them to be friends and lovers while acknowledging their differences. More confusion followed: contraception, while promising new levels of intimacy and eroticism detached from procreation, has provided us with sex without the spiritual or emotional ties that gives the act its meaning. Free sex has become promiscuity, inaugurating an era of date rape, abortions, dehumanizing pornography, and sex without love.

∼

WHILE THE CLINTON SCANDAL commanded the media's attention, a film called *Blast from the Past*, influenced by the swing boom, was relased. It tells the story of Adam Webber, played with winsome innocence by Brendan Fraser. Adam is raised in a bomb shelter for the first thirty-five years of his life, after his eccentric inventor father (Christopher Walken) mistakes a plane crash for the big one during the 1962 Cuban Missile Crisis. In a reversal of the Tarzan fable, Adam is sheltered from the wilds of the outside world and the cultural revolutions of the 1960s and 1970s. He is taught ballroom dancing by mom (Sissy Spacek), boxing by dad, and impeccable manners by both. He learns Latin, French, and German in the shelter's makeshift classroom.

Cut to the 1990s. It's thirty-five years later, long enough for the radiation to dissipate, and Adam's dad ventures to the surface to hunt for survivors. At this point, the film becomes remarkable. Rather than indulge in a predictable fish-out-of-water tale, wherein Adam and his parents are forced to encounter the modern world and are better for their experience (as in the 1997 film *Pleasantville*, which dragged the poor naïfs of the 1950s into modern America), the filmmakers depict modern liberal America as exactly what Adam's father says it is: a toxic purgatory. When Mr. Webber emerges from the shelter he encounters gun-brandishing gang-bangers, New Age religious fanatics, an adult book store where their house once stood, and a transvestite hooker. "It was horrible," Mr. Webber tells his wife after beating a hasty retreat. "They can change their sex! They're mutants!"

The problem is that Adam is now a young man with desires. His parents decide to send him to the surface for supplies and to find a wife. Once up, Adam encounters Eve, a thoroughly modern woman. Promiscuous, terrified of commitment, unwilling to settle for anyone who isn't a jerk, she rejects Adam, turned off by what she sees as his squareness and goofy, excessive politeness. Praying is "always a good idea," he beams. Adam is stunned to discover that "everyone's divorced," and informs Eve's roommate that "manners are a way of showing other people we respect them." He's de-lighted when he finds out one of Eve's friends is "gay": "Thank you for being happy all the time," Adam tells him. Adam Webber is the anti-Clinton.

But Eve begins to see Adam through the eyes of the ci-vility-starved modern world. While other men are obsessed with her body parts, Adam compliments her eyes. In the film's best scene, his daily dance lessons pay off when they go to a swing club and Adam literally sweeps two beautiful blondes off their feet with his footwork. It dawns on Eve that it isn't Adam who's abnormal, but the culture she lives in. "This street used to be little houses and gardens," her room-mate notes later in the film as they search in a grimy alley behind a porn shop for the entrance to the Webber's bomb shelter. "Boy," Eve replies sarcastically, "we've come a long way."

In the 1960s—or even 1980s—*Blast from the Past* would have been dismissed by liberal critics and pop culture watch-ers as reactionary, possibly even fascist. Yet with the resur-gence in swing's popularity it seems a new ethos has taken hold of the popular culture—or at least a small part of it. Simply by advocating nice dress, traditional gender roles, ci-vility, talented musicians, romanticism, and joy—not to mention adulthood—swing is the first fad that has kids look-ing to grandparents and traditional rules for what's hip. In such small ways will the culture war be won.

This is no small thing. In an essay called "Notes on the Culture Wars," Richard John Neuhaus noted that "culture is the way we live, and the way we live in argument with the way we think we ought to live. It has to do with what we eat, wear, watch, admire, and abhor. It has to do with dating, and marriage, and raising children, and trying to get a grasp on what it means to live a good life before our lives are over... whether the Fed raises the interest rate or there is a Democratic Senate pales in importance by comparison with whether Junior is on drugs or if his father is seeing that other woman." Swing is nothing less than a pop culture revolt against the youth culture of the last forty years.

Of course, it's also unbelievable fun. About two months after I started dancing, I was at Glen Echo when it happened —my first swing-related high. I was twirling my partner to a jump blues number—I think it was "Good Rockin' Tonight"—when my consciousness seemed to take off. I felt lighter, yet at the same time completely sure on my feet. Hoots of delight came from my mouth, and my partner laughed along. I later discovered that my experience is somewhat common among dancers as well as athletes. As far back as 1922, anthropologist A. R. Radcliffe-Brown described similar euphoria among those who dance in religious rituals: "As the dancer loses himself in the dance, as he becomes absorbed in the unified community, he reaches a state of elation in which he feels himself filled with energy or force immediately beyond his ordinary state, and so finds himself able to perform prodigies of exertion." Athletes describe such feelings of euphoria as being "in the zone." As former NFL great Joe Greene once put it, "It's almost like being possessed. [But while] it is a kind of frenzy, of wild action . . . you are never out of control. You have great awareness of everything that is happening around you and your part in the whole."

It's an amazing, magical feeling, greater than anything offered by the rock 'n' roll culture. And after the first time I experienced it, whatever traces were left of my self-absorbed radicalism disappeared.

FOUR

Phony Rebels

New York World-Telegram and Sun

Elvis: A revolutionary?

I N JUNE OF 1998, just a few months after the Gap adver-
tisment had set off a jitterbug craze in America, there
was a major culture clash at Zones, a club in downtown
Washington, D.C. On the fifth floor of the club, in the room
featuring swing dancing, a young woman who didn't know
how to dance came face to face with Tom Koerner. Although
the young woman didn't know how to jitterbug, she was on
the dance floor bouncing around new-wave style, head bob-
bing. Most of the beer in her glass was splashing on the floor
—a potential hazard for dancers.

"I told her to get off the floor," Koerner recalls. "She kind
of laughed and mock-threw her beer at me, but then she
moved. Good thing she didn't toss that beer, 'cause I would
have hit her. I would have hit her in a second."

On its face, this incident would seem to be a total betrayal
of the new swing ethic. Here was a man bullying a woman
when the swing lifestyle claims to be a throwback to more
civilized, chivalrous times. But the contradiction is only ap-
parent. In the heyday of swing, people seemed to know how
to behave, and the new swing movement is trying to recap-
ture those timeless mores. At the Savoy, part of the floor,

called "the cat's corner," was reserved for the best dancers, and anyone without the dancing chops who trespassed on that part of the floor would be ostracized, or even take a beating. If a drunk woman had ventured onto the main part of the Savoy's gigantic floor without a partner and danced by herself, sending most of her drink everywhere but her mouth, she would have been escorted out of the club.

In the post-1960s American rock 'n' roll culture, of course, there were no longer supposed to be any hierarchies or social norms. It wasn't just radical urban politicians like Marion Barry who were justifying antinomianism in the name of a socialist-inspired egalitarianism; the spoiled white kids of suburbia also rejected elitism as the ultimate sin. Even if they were from the wealthy suburbs, these were rock 'n' roll kids raised on sitcom morality and MTV. Clubs were for doing whatever you wanted; dance floors were for "moshing," a crude, atavistic form of near-rioting in which kids rush into each other like bumper cars.

When Koerner ordered the yuppie off the floor at Zones, it was a highly symbolic and significant act. Unlike swing havens such as Los Angeles's Derby or Washington's Glen Echo, Zones was a downtown nightclub that for years—and under a different name—was filled with artificial smoke and techno music rather than suspenders and saddle shoes. But in 1998 the swing revival was burrowing into the strongholds of rock and showing no signs of stopping. In the coming months, several other swing clubs would open in D.C., and hundreds were popping up all over the country.

～

ODDLY, SOME PEOPLE HAVE CLAIMED that the new swing is part of the continuing rock 'n' roll revolution rather than a reaction to it. The day after the death of Frank Sinatra, an icon to many in the new swing scene, MTV veejay Matt Pinfield went on the air and called Ol' Blue Eyes "the first punk." To many of the gatekeepers of rock's traditions, punk rock, the blaring, rude, art-school inspired antimusic fad of the 1970s, is the touchstone for all the cool rock music that followed. Lumping Sinatra with the Sex Pistols was a high compliment, at least among the tyrannically hip MTV staff.

Around the same time, the book *Swing! The New Retro Renaissance* also tried to draw swing into the punk fold. Author V. Vale explains that neo-swing began in the late 1980s, led by California bands like Royal Crown Revue and Big Bad Voodoo Daddy. While the bands worship Count Basie, Louis Jordan, and Sinatra, they also sport tatoos and earrings and claim to have been influenced by punk bands like the Sex Pistols and Black Flagg (which may explain why they play so fast and many dancers don't consider them swing bands at all). These bands are, according to Vale, "the "new punk."

Hence, MTV's retroactive "elevation" of Sinatra. "Having passed through the initial howl of the Beats, the 'tune-in, turn-on, drop-out' resistance of the Hippies, and the complete anti-authoritarianism of Punk, what new form of social and cultural rebellion could possibly emerge?," Vale asks. The answer? "Ironically enough, it is a movement that uses the very same society it criticizes as a reference point: the retro-swing movement."

It is a sad sign of the times that we have been so brain-washed by 1960s and punk notions of counterculturalism that absolutely every pop culture fad must be construed as a rebellion against conformity, even when the fad in question is a mad rush back into the arms of tradition. Vale never fully explains just how the neo-swing movement criticizes society from the left. Instead, he uses a lot of academic buzzwords and generally sounds like a college sophomore trying to impress his sociology professor. He launches predictable liberal broadsides at the modern "major media" and at the "jingoism" of an earlier America and indulges in some opaque theorizing about the late twentieth century's "depression of the spirit." He tries to connect these existential dots to dancing, but it doesn't work. Crippled by AIDS, information overload, anxiety, and alienation, people, he posits, are starting to swing and dress sharp as a form of 1960s-style social protest. We don't dance the lindy hop and wear fedoras and saddle shoes to look good or have fun or hear great music. No, it's all a form of rebellion against "the machine."

To be sure, there are liberals in the swing movement. Debra Sternberg describes herself as one and notes that she and Tom Koerner are not religious people. Lavay Smith and her Red Hot Skillet Lickers, the best of the neo-swing bands, hold pro-abortion "swing-for-choice" concerts, and Smith herself is a vegetarian. But they and the swing movement they champion seem to be a throwback to a New Deal–style liberalism. As Fred Siegel notes in *The Future Once Happened Here*, New Deal liberalism offered support for unions, the poor, and minorities but expected moral accountability in return. It upheld decorum and responsibility while fighting for justice; it dressed well and had manners.

In an article in the *Wall Street Journal*, Julia Vitullo-Martin wrote that "today's dancers may be a little punk and a little Goth in dress, but they mostly embrace old dance social principles of courtesy and graciousness." Indeed, if swing is anything, it's a repudiation of the punk aesthetic Vale champions. To understand why this irritates rock fans, it's necessary to deconstruct some widely accepted rock 'n' roll myths repeated reflexively by rock journalists and fans, which constitute a kind of religious dogma in American culture.

Once upon a time, the story goes, America was an innocent, socially cohesive place where children were seen and not heard. Then, in 1955, the sky cracked open, and down came Elvis Presley. Presley was sexual anarchy loosed upon the world, the prime mover in the forty-year rebellion against crushing middle class values. According to *The Rough Guide to Rock*, Elvis "seemed to appear fully formed" from out of the earth. Defiantly wiggling his hips at staid, bourgeois America, he "was the first to present rock 'n' roll not as a dance party but as the soundtrack of alienated youth." Both liberals and conservatives have bought this myth. On page one of his jeremiad *Slouching Towards Gomorrah*, conservative Robert Bork mentions Elvis along with James Dean and the Beats as "harbingers of a new culture that would shortly burst upon us and sweep us into a different country."

This is a captivating story, part of the gospel of the rock establishment. It's also entirely bogus, ignoring both the true origins of rock 'n' roll and the vitality of the swing era, which had more style than rock could ever dream of. If Elvis simply conjured the music he played out of whole cloth, then so did Sinatra. What Elvis played was simply his own version of the gospel, hillbilly, and jump blues that had grown out of swing and which he had listened to growing up in Memphis. And his sound was hardly original. According to James Collier's *Jazz: The American Theme Song*, jump blues began in 1936 with a Chicago group called the Harlem Hamfats—two brothers, Joe and Charles McCoy, who had grown up playing the Mississippi blues. But in 1936 swing was on the rise, and the McCoys' manager decided to bolster their sound by backing them with a hard-swinging New Orleans jazz band. The result was a hard-driving style that was so ebullient that soon other groups began playing "rhythm and blues" style, most famously Louis Jordan and the Tympany Five and Bill Haley of "Rock Around the Clock" fame.

From jump blues, it was a small step to Elvis: "The line from the jazz-based music of the Harlem Hamfats to Elvis Presley," writes Collier, "is astonishingly direct." Early Elvis covers like "That's All Right, Mama," "Good Rockin' Tonight," "Mystery Train," and "Flip, Flop and Fly" were simply jump blues with a hillbilly influence, nothing new or radical—and definitely for dancing, despite what the *Rough Guide* claims. This fact was verified by Elvis himself in 1956, when he mulled over why what he was doing was causing such a fuss: "The colored folks been singing it and playing it just like I'm doin' it now, man, for more years than I know. They played it like that in their shanties and their juke joints, and nobody paid no mind 'til I goosed it up."

Aside from swing, there was another thing Elvis and many of the early rockers had in common with black artists: they were heavily inspired by Christianity. In fact, the musical blurring of lines between the secular and sacred is as old as American popular music itself. The early immigrants brought their musical traditions to the New World with them, whether they were New England Protestants singing British hymns, Irish Catholics enjoying Celtic folk songs, or slaves from Africa and the West Indies performing the polyrhythmic drumming. These styles came together in New Orleans more than in any other place. At the time of the Louisiana Purchase in 1803, New Orleans was a city of ten thousand— half black and half white. Since Louisana had been owned by the Spanish and the French, the official religion was Catholic. Unlike the Protestant settlers who would arrive in New

Orleans after the Louisiana Purchase, the Catholic leaders in the city did not prohibit drumming and dancing. When the steady rhythm of African drumming clashed with the European tradition of the marching band, a new kind of music was formed—jazz. At the same time, a hybridization had taken place between African and European folk music forms, thanks largely to the Great Awakening of 1800. After the American Revolution insured freedom of speech, preachers flocked from the Northeast to the South, many of them abolitionists preaching equality between the races. At camp revival meetings throughout the country, the European religious folk hymn became, as music historian Marshall Stearns puts it, "Africanized." Rhythm and a call-and-response from preacher to congregation were added.

The mix of cultures was taking place outside of church as well. Blacks idioms like the blues, the work song, and spirituals were increasingly heard by whites, thanks largely to minstrelsy. As Donald Clark points out in his comprehensive *The Rise and Fall of American Popular Music*, minstrelsy began as a racist joke, with whites putting on black face to sing black songs, but it led to black music being heard and appreciated by whites. Between the minstrels, the revival meetings, and the marching bands of New Orleans, which were heard increasingly in the North as jazz moved up the Mississippi River, a new form of American music was emerging. The marching beat of New Orleans evolved into swing, which was the forefather of rock 'n' roll.

Still, somehow the mythology has arisen that Elvis was unprecedented, raunchy, sinful. "Elvis's sinfulness brought him alive," once wrote left-wing rock critic Greil Marcus. But as Steve Turner notes in his absorbing *Hungry for Heaven: Rock 'n' Roll and the Search for Redemption*, Elvis had frequently visited East Trigg Baptist Church while he was growing up, where he saw Marion Williams, Mahalia Jackson, and other gospel greats. (Another regular visitor was a young boy named B. B. King.) Elvis himself was a member of the Pentecostal church, as was Jerry Lee Lewis. Other "pioneers" of rock 'n' roll were also Christians and churchgoers. Chuck Berry, Buddy Holly, and Little Richard were Baptists.

Of course, as Turner points out, this doesn't mean that any of these men were the most pious members of the congregation, or even that they went to church frequently. What it does mean, however, is that as well as being Christians who grew up hearing gospel music, they were acutely aware of the concept of sin and ambivalent about playing what many of their preachers told them was the devil's music.

∽

ALTHOUGH ELVIS WASN'T FAR REMOVED from swing music, it might have seemed that way because of the strange direction jazz had taken beginning in the late 1940s. In 1947 at a club in Harlem named Minton's, a group of musicians began experimenting with a new approach to jazz music. Bandleader Teddy Hill formed a house band with trumpeters Kenny Clarke and Dizzy Gillespie and pianist Thelonious Monk. During nightly jam sessions others would join them, most notably alto sax great Charlie Parker, who had gotten his start in the swing bands of Kansas City.

Vats of ink have been spilled in deciphering their music, known as bebop. It's something that, if jazz writers are to be believed, defies easy categorization. Nevertheless, a succinct four-part summary was offered by Neil Tesser in his 1998 *Playboy Guide to Jazz*. First, the beboppers used small, quick combos instead of orchestras, relying most often on five pieces: trumpet and saxophone, backed by piano, bass, and drums. Second, the musicians used more complex chords, exploring "lively, colorful combinations of notes that previous listeners considered too dissonant for jazz." Third, beboppers often abandoned the melody of a song in order to improvise, relying more heavily on the song's harmony. Fourth, the beboppers had attitude: "Instead of smooth and hummable melodies designed for dancing, the beboppers created angular tunes with unexpected accents and irregular phrases—and they expected people to listen, rather than jitterbug, to these songs and the solos that followed. The boppers emerged as jazz's first 'angry young men.' They saw themselves as artists first and entertainers second, and they demanded that others respect them and their music accordingly."

This was a far cry from crowd-pleasers Duke Ellington, Cab Calloway, and Glenn Miller. This isn't to say that the new jazz music wasn't brilliant; many of the albums from that era are classics that seem only to acquire more appeal with age. Albums like *Art Blakey and the Jazz Messengers*, saxophone great Dexter Gordon's *Go!*, saxophonist Sonny Rollins's *Vol. 2*, and John Coltrane's *Blue Train* are timeless, bristling with energy, jaw-dropping improvisation, and the deep spirituality of great jazz.

The problem wasn't the music, but that these musicians were too full of themselves, rejecting the notion that jazz could ever be accessible pop music as well as art. Bebop offered challenges musicians thought they could never get from traditional swing bands, as well as an improvisational ethic that provided an escape from the obligation of writing strong melodies. The big bands evaporated, and before long anyone who had been in a swing band became a joke to the beboppers. Producer Quincy Jones once recalled that as a young musician he hid backstage from bebop trumpeter Miles Davis so that Davis wouldn't know that Jones was in the swing band that had just left the stage. Moreover, bebop was impossible to dance to, and the alienation many of the musicians felt from Eisenhower's America become a beacon to intellectuals and bohemians. Even bebop's founders weren't safe from the ideological putsch: when bebop master Charlie Parker made an album of pop standards with a band backed up with a string section, he was called a sell-out by "forward-looking" jazz purists.

All of these factors signalled the end of jazz as a popular art form. Gone were the days when five thousand people would fill the Savoy Ballroom in Harlem to lindy hop to the sunny sounds of Ella Fitzgerald or Count Basie. Swing morphed into rhythm and blues then rock 'n' roll, and the kids followed. The audience for jazz shrank. Beboppers and their fans still blame the decline of jazz's popularity on racism. Miles Davis once called pop music "white music," and Kareem Abdul-Jabarr, in a jazz documentary, offers that jazz didn't sell because "whites couldn't appreciate anything that came from black culture."

Yet these same "whites" had sent Ella Fitzgerald, Count Basie, and other black swing artists to the top of the charts. Only two kinds of music were allowed on the radio following the news of FDR's death: classical music and a concert by Duke Ellington. Something other than Jim Crow was responsible for jazz's popular failure: the music itself. No one was writing great melodies, the heart and soul of pop music and what record buyers look for. Beboppers' explorations into harmony produced stunning innovations, but it was all meat and potatoes, no ice cream. In popularity, they couldn't touch the jump blues of Little Richard or hillbilly swing of Elvis—not to mention the equally successful Sinatra, who recorded a series of classic, highly melodic jazz-pop albums in the 1950s.

This split had nothing to do with racism. In his 1998 book of essays *Always in Pursuit*, the unflinching black jazz critic Stanley Crouch included a piece on Duke Ellington, whose centennial was celebrated in 1999. Ellington, the greatest jazz composer who ever lived, was also, Crouch writes, like many Negro jazz innovators, a favored child. He shared with Coleman Hawkins, Charlie Parker, Thelonious Monk, Miles Davis and others a background in which he was pampered, tucked in, read to, and reared to believe in himself and his own opinions without reservation. Our simple-minded presumptions about color and consciousness frequently dupe us into missing the facts of these matters. The restrictions of race had nothing to do with how these artists saw themselves when accurate expression of their imaginations demanded that they innovate.

Crouch also tells a funny story about Ellington that sums up the problems jazz has had finding an audience since the bebop revolution. In the 1960s bassist Charles Mingus suggested to Ellington that they make an "avant-garde" record together, employing some of the chaotic elements in popular in the "free jazz" movement of the time. Ellington replied that he had no desire to take jazz *that* far back.

So if the popular music of the 1950s wasn't quite the revolution it's reputed to have been, when did the music change? How did we go from "Rock Around the Clock" to gansta rap? The best answer is provided by Martha Bayles, whose *Hole in Our Soul: The Loss of Beauty and Meaning in American Popular Music* should be required reading for every rock critic. According to Bayles, the Elvis phenomenon wasn't as much about American teenagers shattering the hypocritical and unnatural constraints of their parents—although Bayles does concede that Elvis represented an acceptable version of black

entertainers and that this was groundbreaking for its time—
as it was about dancing. By the time Elvis came along in the
mid-1950s, the swing bands had been largely replaced by
crooners like Bing Crosby, Perry Como, and Doris Day, but
the kids wanted to dance. Any cursory examination of the
experience of Elvis's first fans will reveal that none of them
was interested in overturning social mores as much as they
just wanted to have some fun on the dance floor.

Bayles also recaptures the Christian roots of rock 'n' roll
from the modern rock academics. She brilliantly dissects the
work of Greil Marcus, the Berkeley professor who is one the
most respected wags in rock's critical establishment. In
Mystery Train, his book on Elvis Presley, Marcus repeats the
contemporary rock myth of Elvis as ur-rebel. He paints
American culture, as Bayles puts it, "as a battleground between puritanical repressiveness and the erotic liberation
promised by art." It was, thinks Marcus, the "secret revolt"
against puritanism that erupted in Elvis's hips. Before Elvis,
writes Marcus, America was, at least musically, a silent place.
On this point, Bayles dispatches Marcus with ease:

> The speediest way to refute [Marcus's] thesis is to point
> out that it sidesteps practically the entire history of
> Afro-American music. Marcus says nothing about
> plantation music, spirituals, minstrelsy, ragtime, jazz,
> gospel, or swing. . . . In the end Marcus takes an oddly
> bifurcated view of Afro-American music—a view that

is, unfortunately, quite prevalent today. On the one hand, he praises "black music" as a source for rock 'n' roll, depicting Presley as the Prometheus who stole its spark, passing it to the white race as it languished in frigid puritanism. On the other, he refuses to regard Afro-American music as a living competitor to his beloved rock 'n' roll. His whole argument implies that nothing of any real musical significance occurred between the founding of the Jamestown colony and the release of "That's All Right, Mama."

Marcus also attempts to take the religion out of Elvis, acknowledging that religion is at the root of the genre he celebrates while targeting it as the very thing Elvis represented escape from. According to Marcus, Presley's "sinfulness brought him to life," and he represented the hope that joy and abandon can last "as Saturday fades into Monday." As Bayles notes, "typically, Marcus restructures the week so that Saturday fades into Monday instead of Sunday, the day when enthusiasm gets put to non-hedonistic uses. Ruled out of bounds is the possibility of an enthusiasm that subsumes or transcends the erotic."

According to Bayles, the real shift in American popular music didn't come in the 1950s, with Elvis, but in the 1960s. It was in that decade, writes Bayles, that the positive, funny, sensual, and spiritual idioms of African-American musical traditions collided with "perverse modernism," which Bayles defines as "the antiart impulses of the European avant-garde, which gave rise historically to such movements as decadence at the end of the nineteenth century; futurism at the start of the twentieth; dada in the 1920s; surrealism and the theater of cruelty in the 1930s; and postwar retreads of these movements, such as happening and performance art in the 1950s and 60s." These influences came into rock 'n' roll when young Britons who were the products of that country's art schools began playing American music. The most famous practitioners were the Rolling Stones, who began as a third-rate blues cover band and quickly gained fame as the dirtier and more menacing alternative to the Beatles. The Stones quickly gained fame through their rudeness to their own audience, iconoclastic behavior, and Mick Jagger's cross-dressing, antics that are regarded as part of rock's grand tradition, but in reality had nothing to do with the positive spirituality of American pop music forms.

After the Stones, other bands followed suit: Led Zeppelin, which took the subtlety of the blues and regurgitated it as pounding, nightmarish heavy metal; Frank Zappa and the Mothers of Invention, who excelled more in sarcasm than in scales; and the Velvet Underground, less a band than a theater troupe. The plaything of Andy Warhol, who hired the band to play at a 1966 happening, the Velvet Underground's members were Lou Reed, a poet inspired by the Beats, avant-garde musician John Cale, and a German model named Nico. While the band's music was insipid, by this time music was almost beside the point—especially when you were being compared to Berlin Cabaret, as the Velvet was.

While the Velvet Underground wasn't a popular success, its impact on popular music has been incalculable. One of the rock clichés that does contain some truth is the saying that while the Velvet Underground didn't sell many records, everyone who bought one formed a band. Perhaps the best student was Malcolm McLaren, a young English fashion shop owner who had been to no less than six art schools. In the mid-1970s McLaren formed a band called the Sex Pistols. The Pistols were based both on the neo-marxist French "situationism," which advocated the use of mass media for revolutionary purposes, and punk rock, a marginialized form of rebel music being played in New York City. Punk was reaction to the blandness of disco and the increasingly arty pretentions of rock; it offered bands like the Ramones, who played fast, loud, and short pop songs. But when punk was co-opted by McLaren it became some thing else: an all-out assault on the senses.

While at the time it was considered a freak accident by the mainstream rock establishment, punk did not stay underground for long. Indeed, it became the inspiration for an entirely new generation of musicians. Elvis Costello, the Jam, the Clash (English marxists who named an album *Sandinista!*), the Dead Kennedys, and scores of others all adopted punk's confrontational sneer, even if some groups mixed the attitude with softer and more traditional forms of pop song-writing and called it New Wave. Then in 1991 the dam burst: a punk band named Nirvana came out with an album, *Nevermind*, that sold ten million copies. Punk, now called "grunge" or "alternative," was king.

In one sense, the punk revolution was welcome. By the mid-1970s rock had grown corpulent with self-satisfaction and phony, drug-induced mysticism, and a benefit of punk's sandblasting was that one of its prime targets was the narcissism of the hippies. Yet the downside was worse: much of the music was intolerable, and as punk gained in dominance, young music fans began to forget that popular music had once been about something other than transgression. Their amnesia was encouraged by the rock press and liberal elite, which defended, for example, the Sex Pistol's spitting on their audience by claiming that it was just the next chapter in the tradition that began with Elvis's shocking the audience on the *Ed Sullivan Show*. And spirituality, which had been so central to pop music since it's inception, was obliterated: "I am the Antichrist," the Pistols' Johnny Rotten ranted in the punk anthem "Anarchy in the UK."

Today, the "revolutionary" changes wrought in the 1960s have become the status quo, the rituals of rock boring and predictable. When a young misanthrope smashes his guitar on stage at a punk show, it's about as shocking as a saxophone solo during the big band era. Rebellion and alienation are the common stances—so common they have all but run out of targets for their rage. In short, what has happened to the other forms of art in the twentieth century has happened to popular music. In the Spring 1997 issue of the *Public Interest*, Roger Kimball describes the transformation of art from a medium grounded in spirituality that celebrated beauty to a political forum whose only purpose seems to be transgressing every moral and aesthetic boundary. Kimball documents the rise of modern art from the margins of the counterculture to the dominant model of expression. As Kimball notes, "the avant-garde has become a casualty of its own success. Having won battle after battle, it gradually transformed a recalcitrant bourgeois culture into a willing collaborator in its raids on establishment taste."

∾

IN THE SUMMER OF 1998, it seemed that rock's hegemony might actually be weakening. Swing was everywhere: the top-forty charts, videos, commercials. Some nights Glen Echo had lines and turned away hundreds. CNN interviewed me and followed me out dancing.

In such a perfervid atmosphere, it is easy to forget how strong, pervasive, and powerful the rock culture has become. In July of 1998 I attended a rally following the Tibetan Freedom Concert, which had attracted tens of thousands of young do-gooders to Washington, D.C. The repression of Tibet by the Chinese was a hot political issue on the rock 'n' roll left, and the concert easily attracted a capacity crowd, filling the fifty-five-thousand-seat RFK stadium. Despite its claims of high purpose, the concert was nothing more than a mutual affirmation session: I stand for something, therefore I am. As John Dugan said of the Freedom Concert in the *Washington City Paper*: "I've come to believe that Tibet symbolizes much more for some of these followers: a quest for new meaning and a chance to redefine themselves."

In this sense, nothing has changed since the 1960s. Almost twenty years ago, Christopher Lasch beat Dugan to the punch when he summed up the atmosphere in post-1960s America: "The contemporary climate is therapeutic, not religious. People today hunger not for personal salvation, let alone for the restoration of an earlier golden age, but for the feeling, the momentary illusion, of personal well-being, health, and psychic security. Even the radicalism of the sixties served, for many of those who embraced it for personal rather than political reasons, not as a substitute religion but as a form of therapy. Radical politics filled empty lives, provided a sense of meaning and purpose." Lasch then uses the radical 1960s group the Weathermen as an example, noting that "the atmosphere in which the Weathermen lived—an atmosphere of violence, danger, drugs, sexual promiscuity, moral and psychic chaos—derived not so much from an older revolutionary tradition as from the turmoil and narcissistic anguish of contemporary America."

That narcissistic anguish is now the property of a new generation of phony rebels, and watching them cover Capitol Hill during the rally made me realize that more people had gone to the concert that day than would go dancing at Glen Echo in a year. The kids at the Tibet rally—and those at the anti–World Bank protest in Seattle—had the same imprecise "rage against the machine," the same obsession with being hip while trying to act aloof, the same hypocritical hatred of the middle-class values, whose benefits they continue to enjoy, as the protestors in the 1960s. Their comments, whether on MTV or in the *Washington Post*, revealed the same half-baked activism: "Uh, I read some pamphlets and it's really bogus what's going on in Tibet, dude. It should stop. When's the next band coming on?"

Still, their numbers were huge. On the way home, I drove through Shaw. Driving past the padlocked Howard Theater, I tried in vain to find some swing on the radio. I realized that in a way I, too, was living in a secret city.

FIVE

It's All About Class

Mary Freeman

Tom Koerner and Debra Sternberg at America.

I N 1998, when neo-swing was peaking, a couple of years after I became a swing dancer, I met Fayard Nicholas, one-half of the greatest dance duo ever to grace an American stage. Nicholas was in a Washington hospital recovering from a stroke; like the swing era he came from, he seemed to be fading. Sitting in a wheelchair, skinny and almost completely bald, but with dancing brown eyes, he had a thin, high-pitched pixie voice that conveyed delight even when he was describing his troubles. When he laughed, which was often, it was with such force that his head dipped and his body bent forward in his wheelchair.

From the 1930s through the 1950s Fayard Nicholas and his brother Harold, six years Fayard's junior, were—with the exception of Fred Astaire—the most famous dancers in America. They were also the best. The sons of Philadelphia musicians, the self-taught brothers began dancing as children. By the early 1930s, when Harold was eight and Fayard was fourteen, they were playing the Cotton Club, where the brothers tapped and sang for two shows a night at midnight and two in the morning. Because the club was run by gangsters, the boys didn't have to worry about child labor laws. In

Jazz Dance, historians Marshall and Jean Stearns described the boys in performance: "Dressed immaculately in top hats and tails, they played at being sophisticated in a way that delighted everyone, and they seemed to radiate joy at being treated like grown-ups." Fayard remembered: "The Nicholas Brothers were always about class."

The brothers went from the Cotton Club to Hollywood, where they became stars and appeared in films like *Kid Millions*, *Sun Valley Serenade*, and *The Great American Broadcast*. Their performance was what dance historians call a "flash act," joining jazz steps with acrobatics to electrifying affect. They combined tap with back flips, twists, and jaw-dropping circus stunts. Their most famous move was taking a ten-foot leap off the stage and landing in the splits. It always brought the house down—though there were some people who dreaded seeing it.

"No one wanted to follow us!" Fayard cried with delight, leaning over to let out the laugh. "We were the showstoppers. There was this one time in Cannes that we were supposed to open for Maurice Chevalier. We got there for rehearsal and the stage manager said to Chevalier, 'Okay, first the Nicholas brothers come out, then you follow.' Chevalier said, 'No, no way. You don't open with the Nicholas Brothers. You close with the Nicholas Brothers.'"

After years of making movies—a total of forty-four—and touring the world, the brothers' popularity declined in the 1950s with the rise of bebop and the death of jazz dancing. After a separation from 1958 to 1964, they reunited, and since then—and despite a double hip replacement for Fayard in 1985—they have played Vegas, entertained the troops with Bob Hope, and done the occasional television special. While a coast has separated them since 1980, when Harold moved to New York, they have never retired. "This is the greatest country in the world," Fayard beamed, "There's so much opportunity!"

~

OF COURSE, IN MODERN AMERICA Fayard and Harold might seem like relics. They have too much class and are far too happy. Driving home after talking to Fayard, I couldn't help noticing that everybody on the street looked like a deadbeat, from the inner-city hip-hoppers with their baggy pants and Raider caps to the suburban grungers in their puke-colored pseudo-1970s garb. The adults didn't look any better. Although blessed with opportunities the Nicholas brothers couldn't have imagined, none of these people looked like they had had fun in years. Yet their misery was selfish and weak— the ennui of the spoiled. Their tacky clothes didn't help.

What a difference from the people who lived during the Depression and the swing era, who knew how to look in public. Even the destitute from that time had class. In a 1999 article in the *Wall Street Journal*, Ned Crabb noted that the childishness of modern dress often provokes childish behavior. He then offered this insight on photographs of the poor from the early part of the century: "Suffering is written on the faces of these men and women and their children, but when we look at them 60 years later, they still bear a fierce dignity, standing there in their threadbare clothes. At least, when the camera captured their images and exposed their suffering for others to gape and wonder at, they weren't wearing fanny packs or backward baseball caps or T-shirts reading 'Beam me up Scotty.'"

These days, people aren't trapped by poverty, but by a culture that sells the tyranny of rebellion and dressing-down as liberation itself. In 1985, science fiction writer Harlan Ellison was asked by *Rolling Stone* to write an essay about the then new all-music television station MTV. After days of watching nothing but music videos, Ellison offered this conclusion: "Rock is freedom. Welcome to the gulag." As Ellison saw it, music video had been a promising new art form which was corrupted by MTV, an organization whose main goal was "to cop an attitude of nihilistic uninvolvement that would make Camus look like an activist." A handful of videos were "damn near art," Ellison wrote, but MTV's adolescent-obsessed junk machine would make sure that those clips were smothered by shots of breaking glass, naked girls, and bad hair. In short, whatever freedom rock had promised had been caged in a silly antiestablishment pose.

This was no more evident than in an essay that appeared in the August 1, 1999, *New York Times*. In "Smart, Lyrical, Even Genteel, but is it Rock?," *Spin* and *Village Voice* hack Eric Weisbard offered what he thought was a fresh and bold thesis: rock 'n' roll has got too nice. What with the lilting country lyricism of singer Lucinda Williams and the safe acts like the Mavericks and the Brian Setzer Orchestra gaining popularity, rock has lost its raison d'être—offending people. "When did it become possible to enter the pantheon alongside Elvis, the Rolling Stones, the Sex Pistols and Nirvana without getting your hands dirty?" Weisbard whined.

A better question might be how the Rolling Stones and punk rock snatched rock 'n' roll from the swing-inspired groups that created it. What swing offers is what rock culture needs: the guts to banish all the inbred, misogynistic mouth-breathers who are worshipped by phony iconoclasts like Weisbard as representatives of "real rock." By the summer of 1999 critics were declaring neo-swing dead, but this might have been wishful thinking by the doyens of rock dissipation. Swing's popularity in the mass media had waned after the explosion caused by the Gap ad, but the lines at places like Glen Echo and the Derby remained long on swing nights, and do so today. What had happened was that swing had caused a lot of sound and fury establishing a beachhead in the popular culture, and once the noise died down critics declared the movement over. But it had simply become another part of the popular culture. It didn't topple the dominant musical culture of aggression, but it has changed lives and continues to offer an alternative.

How badly that alternative is needed became clear in August 1999, during a concert celebrating the thirtieth anniversary of Woodstock. In a tragic, banal, and profligate debacle, the festival ended in a melee of rioting and rape. When

I read in the *Washington Post* that at the beginning of the festival a girl got her genitals pierced and was hoisted in the air by her boyfriend to show people the job, I knew that rock had gone so far in the direction of provoking outrage that it had come full circle to conformity. In his book *The Coming of the Golden Age: A View of the End of Progress*, molecular biologist Gunther Stent recently wrote about the paradox of total freedom locking artists into a box: "The artist's accession to near-total freedom of expression now presents very cognitive difficulties for the appreciation of his work. The absence of recognizable canons reduces his act of creation to near-randomness for the perceiver. In other words, artistic evolution along the one-way street to freedom embodies an element of self-limitation."

This argument is lost on rock's current cheerleaders. Rock music that has been pushed to the extreme, that is at the edge of loud, fast, and abrasive, is, like the cheesy 1950s pop of Patti Page it usurped, torpid and predictable—even, to use that deadliest of words, conservative. Guitars turned up to eleven simply have no where else to go. The same goes for human "freedom," a right valued more highly than any other in today's rock culture. At Woodstock '99, Alanis Morisette was interviewed on MTV. When she was informed that many women in the crowd were going topless and claimed Morrisette as their inspiration, she positively beamed. "I think it's beautiful," she said. "I'm all for people not having any constraints, of being as free as they possibly can." Morisette didn't seem to understand that too much freedom is as limiting as any repression rock music supposedly combats. A fully-dressed woman is a mystery; a young woman in the nude is an open book, a person wearing her narcissism and lack of self-respect on her shoulder. She becomes a one-dimensional object in the eyes of men, who often have only one thing on their minds.

Rock critics celebrate this moral free fall, despite the fact that it's a prison. In his *New York Times* article Eric Weisbard held up raunch-rapper Eminem as an example of what rock 'n' roll needs: "The song on which [Eminem] raps baby talk to his daughter about why he had to murder her mother, sampling his own infant's voice, is pure rock and roll, pushing limits I never knew existed. Gentrify that." One can sense the desperation in Weisbard's voice; rock cannot be entertaining and funny and nice—someone somewhere must be offended. While he claimed this shock of the new is a novel sensation, it's difficult to believe that Weisbard hadn't heard it before—or that he really can't recognize the moral boundary preventing someone from murdering his wife then boasting about it to his daughter.

～

IT IS THIS KIND OF THING that led conservative political activist Paul Weyrich, in 1999, to publish an open letter which declared that America is no longer a moral country. Despite lying under oath and sexual misconduct and impeachment, President Clinton had remained in office, a fact that sent

Weyrich into despair. "What Americans would have found absolutely intolerable only a few years ago," he wrote, "a majority not only tolerates but celebrates." He would be backed up by Roger Kimball of the *New Criterion*: "At the deepest level," Kimball wrote, "at the level of the culture's taken-for-granted feelings and assumptions about what matters—the hedonistic, self-infatuated ethos of cultural revolution has triumphed to an extent unimaginable when it began." *National Journal*'s Michael Kelly put it more bluntly: "The Marxist ideal is at last reached. We live, finally, in a classless society: No one has any class at all."

Weyrich even suggested that in response to the moral chaos that had taken over the United States, conservatives retreat, building their own neighborhoods and institutions separate from mainstream culture. He suggested, in other words, building a secret city—something like a neoconservative version of Shaw, Washington's long-forgotten city within a city.

If such a place were built, it might resemble 1940s and 1950s America, which would not be an entirely bad thing. It's become a modern mantra, repeated by both left and right, that "we don't want to go back" to pre-1960s America—as if that would be tantamount to erasing the Enlightenment. But prerevolutionary America might not have been as poisonous—or as banal—as people think. It was, after all, a place whose culture catered to adult tastes. In *Swingin' at the Savoy*, Norma Miller recalls that in the 1930s and 1940s Harlem was a big adult playground, where people could "crawl all night." The country as a whole seemed more enchanting: there were literate radio shows, musicals on the stage, swing bands, dance halls, and movies that entertained by depicting adults doing adult things. It was also a world open to teenagers, even if that term didn't exist. Back then, they were "young people," and if they did any rebelling it wasn't because their parents didn't understand their culture but because they, the teenagers, wanted to be part of the adult world.

In the book *Teenagers: An American History*, Grace Palladino recounts a telling episode that occurred in 1941 in Washington, D.C., when a group of teenaged girls skipped their field trip to the National Gallery of Art to catch a movie starring the Glen Miller Orchestra. When they returned they found their classmates had gone, leaving the girls to go to a police station to wait for a ride home. According to reports at the time, while they waited, the girls "jitterbugged up and down the corridors," which irritated some of the officers. As Palladino sees it, this episode is just a link in the ageless chain of teen insouciance, evidence that "[Benny] Goodman's bobbysoxers and the Beatles fans [are] part of the same cultural trend." This seems like a clever cultural observation, but it widely misses the mark. Diana West, in a review of *Teenagers* for the *New Criterion*, made an obvious observation: "It's worth noting that the movie [the girls ditched the gallery to see], a bit of fluff called *Sun Valley Serenade* [featuring the Nicholas brothers], portrays the Miller band performing 'In the Mood,' an archetypal swing number, for a black-tie, adult crowd. . . . [The film] is by no means a 'teen' movie: the imagery, the style, the context, all relate to an adult world."

And that adult world was a dancing world. In his book *1939: The Lost World of the Fair*, David Gelernter takes the reader on a tour of an America that before neo-swing was thought to have vanished. It was a place, he writes, where people danced:

> Of course I mean serious dancing as 1939 understood it: in time to the music, the right steps in the right sequence, with due regard to the social conventions and wherever possible, cheek to cheek. And 1939 favored serious dances: the occasional waltz or fox trot, yes, but also the hectic jitterbug, the complex rumba and still more complicated samba. By 1940 there must have been close to two hundred dance orchestras in the United States; every last one of them wanted to play Manhattan.
>
> . . . . .
>
> All over this serious city, people dance. They dance at the Rainbow Room, "where society, celebrities and men of affairs entertain." They dance at the Stork Club: "plenty popular, plenty atmosphere, plenty expensive." They dance at Roseland and El Morocco. They dance at Leon & Eddie's ("most famous cabaret nightclub in the country") and the Savoy Ballroom in the center of Harlem and at "200 Beautiful Dancing Partners 25 cents Admission 25 cents" on Broadway and at the Arcadia, where tickets are ten cents a dance with one of

the "professional hostesses"—seven cents to the lady and three to the house. They dance at dinner, cocktail hour and even (in a few hotels) at lunch. They dance to Eddie Duchin at the Plaza, Guy Lombardo at the Roosevelt, "high-class music" at the Iridium Room and (on a lucky night) to Benny Goodman at the Pennsylvania. Even the hotels which have no pretension to smartness have wonderful bands. They dance at the beach. They dance in the schools. They dance in their living rooms. . . . If this city is roaring forward (it is!), joy and passion are the fuel and the engine is dance.

New York wasn't the only jumping town. There was Shaw, of course, but also places like Kansas City. Although largely forgotten as such, in the 1930s Kansas City was a town electric with night life and jazz. Count Basie, who learned his way around a piano there before making it in New York, once told an interviewer that he had "never seen anything like" Kansas City in the 1930s. "There was [jazz and blues] coming out of every doorway," he recalled. The bands in Kansas City played all night. Mary Lou Williams, the great jazz pianist who made her name in Kansas City, once recalled that she would finish playing her set and go home to shower and change. As she left for home she would hear the band launch into a long jam, which often involved the different soloists trying to outdo each other. After showering, changing, and eating, she would return to the club, and the band would still be playing the same song.

~

FOLLOWING THE WAR, that world—the dancing, night life "crawling," and adults finding release in extended jazz jams that lasted all night—began to disappear. According to *Teenagers*, the regression began in 1944, when a grandmother named Helen Valentine launched *Seventeen* magazine. Valentine convinced retailers and manufacturers to target the teen audience, and soon it was only a matter of time: in Diana West's phrase, *Seventeen* ushered in "the advent of a brand-new, heretofore unseen, emphasis on—indeed, domination of—the teen experience in mainstream popular culture.... as consumerism became the American pastime, and as consumption . . . became driven by the infantile yearnings of adolescents, the influence of the adult on taste and behavior rapidly diminished."

West gets it almost right. Adult influence did indeed diminish, but not as rapidly as she thinks. It managed to retain a foothold until the 1960s and the ascendance of the baby boomers. My parents, members of the "Silent Generation" that were too young to serve in World War II but too old to be boomers, were in their twenties when they got married in the 1950s, and the world they lived in bore little resemblance to the one that would emerge ten years later. In his book *The Lost City: The Forgotten Virtues of Community in America*, Alan Ehrenhalt examines the popular culture of America in the 1950s—specifically, the black Chicago neighborhood of Bronzeville, a mecca for adults looking for grown-up entertainment. Bronzeville was Chicago's equivalent of Harlem and Shaw, boasting dozens of clubs where legendary performers like Cab Calloway, Duke Ellington, and Nat King Cole played. The local paper, the *Chicago Defender*, even ran a gossip column on the club scene called "While the Squares Sleep."

One particular Bronzeville hot spot, the Roberts Show Lounge, was described as "the biggest Negro-owned nightclub in America." Boasting a thousand seats, it booked Sarah Vaughan, Billy Eckstine, and Sammy Davis Jr. But music was only part of its business, as Ehrenhalt points out:

> Something was going on at the Roberts every day of the week. Even more important than its big-name entertainment policy was its status as a party center for the plethora of social clubs that existed in Bronzeville through the 1950s. [A resident] estimates that there were more than two thousand such clubs, covering most of the economic spectrum from the working class to the elite, and the Roberts was in effect their clubhouse. It was booked months in advance for Sunday afternoon fashion shows and cocktail parties sponsored by one club or another.

There was even life in the whitebread suburbs. Ehrenhalt interviews some of the first residents of the suburb Elmhurst. One woman describes how they would all gather to play volleyball, assured that, because the back windows of their houses faced the field, they could hear if anyone's kid started crying. Another woman who lived around the corner described life this way: "We had great parties. We had parties at least every weekend. We'd have the greatest progressive parties, moving from one house to another. And everyone would drink. People would call the police when we had our parties. We were out in the yard doing the choo-choo train. The police would tell us not to worry about it."

And the fun, at least in my parents' case, didn't end with the arrival of children or the onset of middle age. I was my parents' fourth child, yet as a boy in the late 1970s, when my parents were in their fifties, I remember getting dressed up on weekends to go out for a play, a road trip, or a party. My father used to sponsor a dance called "The Very Senior Prom," where he would hire the Glen Miller Orchestra and throw a huge bash, jitterbugging with his friends while I was home watching television. On New Year's Eve they would stay out all night, coming home after a sunrise breakfast at one of our neighbors' homes. While I had to outgrow heavy metal, then punk, then rap, they stuck with Tommy Dorsey, Sinatra, and Gershwin. They were the last generation raised without television and with artists and musicians who catered to adult tastes. They felt comfortable with pop culture because they were its main audience.

In the 1960s, with the arrival of millions of baby-boom teenagers, the rise of the suburb—which, as Ehrenhalt admits, couldn't keep up its social life for long because of its lack of cultural spots—and the arrival of the Beatles, once-thriving, urban, adult popular culture was overshadowed by the passive culture of television and the youth-oriented rock 'n' roll movement. The new pop culture wasn't catastrophic in and of itself—the Beatles, after all, were brilliant musicians. What was tragic was the devastating, Hiroshima-like completeness with which kid pop eradicated adult pop, leaving no room for evolution. Unlike previous generations, the boomers didn't graduate from the Beatles to Bach or Ella Fitzgerald, from little league to community volleyball, from the twist to the waltz. Lacking even the mild social spunk of the 1950s suburban boozehounds Ehrenhalt describes, the boomers, like their yippie-turned-yuppie peer Jerry Rubin, delved into self-help, therapy, and career, never filling the adult civic and pop culture voids they had created. The major media followed suit: suddenly there were no longer *Playhouse Theater* and jazz on CBS and classical musicians on *Ed Sullivan*; there was the all-important youth market, with its deep pockets—and everyone else. Urban civic and entertainment centers like the Roberts Lounge became rock 'n' roll clubs for the young and stayed that way. Today, it's almost impossible for adults to go out nightclubbing in a city and not feel like they're babysitting.

This disconnection from popular culture for adults, this narcissistic refusal to grow up, is why for the entire 1980s and most of the 1990s, the American media were consistently, relentlessly returning to the 1960s—it's still the only pop culture they have. In 1998, the media turned their gaze to the thirtieth anniversary of 1968, to them the year the world was created. A local station in Washington, D.C., did a multi-part series called *68/98*, a retrospective on the 1960s, which included those underreported stories: Vietnam, Woodstock, and Nixon. Yet 1998 was another anniversary: the sixtieth anniversary of Benny Goodman's historic 1938 swing concert at Carnegie Hall. It was the moment swing first broke into the mainstream. Most of the media were probably unaware of this anniversary, or even who Benny Goodman was.

Then, in April 1998, the Gap ad aired. And if, in the end, the resurgence of swing didn't transform America as completely as some had hoped, it at least offered a respite from the downward spiral of the decadence of post-1960s America. There is a picture above my desk of a group of black swing dancers from Harlem's Savoy in the 1930s, their faces resplendent with joy despite both the Depression and Jim Crow. Like many of today's swingers, the Savoy dancers defied the corruption of the prevailing society through sheer grace and style, refusing to sink under a hostile, oppressive culture. I realize that many will find the comparison of modern conservatives—and old, pro-responsibility New Deal liberals, for that matter—to American blacks of pre-cultural revolution America distasteful, even blasphemous. In the wake of the cultural revolutions that took place in the 1960s, conservatives may be a minority in America, but their status as outsiders is not life-threatening. They are not forced to live in poverty and lynched if they are suspected of committing a crime.

Yet even while acknowledging that the dire conditions faced by blacks in this country are unimaginable to most

Americans today, it's possible to compare the hostility once felt towards blacks and that felt by today's anything-goes culture towards the minority, both black and white, who find offensive teenagers who dress like the homeless, racist rap, crude rock 'n' roll, and jokes about masturbation on primetime television. It's the reticent who now live in a secret city, even if it's psychological, social, and spiritual.

For many, the swing renaissance rekindled hope, offering an uplifting challenge to the "self-infatuated ethos" of modern American life. Everything about swing—its dress, manners, unfiltered fun, and pure joy—contradicts the notion that humanity's problems are the result of racism, homophobia, or lack of therapy, not our own arrogance and narcissism. Swing stands against the kind of "progress" that has brought us suburban sprawl, school shootings, and Madonna.

∼

SWING, IN SHORT, represents a pop movement that for the first time in decades breaks with irony, a guiding principle for rock hacks and other pseudo-rebels throughout the twentieth century. Specifically, swing heralds a break from iconoclastic irony, which Columbia professor Andrew Delbanco explored in his 1995 book, *The Death of Satan: How Americans Have Lost Their Sense of Evil*. According to Delbanco, American irony—the "iconoclastic irony" used to rebel against religion, truth, authority, and everything except irony itself—emerged after World War I. After the bloodbath in

Europe, the American intelligentsia, bolstered by Freud and Nietzsche, rejected Victorian notions about sex, sin, and evil in favor of moral relativism and self-conscious smugness. "Irony was the final polish of the shoe," F. Scott Fitzgerald wrote in 1922, "the ultimate dash of the clothes-brush, a sort of intellectual 'There!'" Fitzgerald called irony "The Holy Ghost of this latter day."

In the 1950s, this antinomianism began to spread and was immortalized in books like *Catch-22* and *The Catcher in the Rye*. The rebellion found its most infamous expression in "The White Negro," an essay by Norman Mailer published in 1954. Mailer celebrated the new aesthetic of "hip," as personified by blacks living in the ghetto. Blacks had been "living on the margin between totalitarianism and democracy for two centuries," Mailer wrote, and their edge lifestyle was the antidote to the boredom of 1950s America. If the options 1950s America offered were death by atomic annihilation or "a slow death by conformity. . . . why then the only life-giving answer is to accept the terms of death . . . [and] to divorce oneself from society, to exist without roots, to set out on that uncharted journey into the rebellious imperatives of the self." Mailer called for people to "encourage the psychopath in [themselves]." It was advice that would be followed by urban rioters in the 1960s and generations of rock 'n' rollers.

Mailer's deeply racist philosophy would become a blueprint for many of the radicals who followed him, from the nihilism of the Weathermen and the drug culture to the degenerate rage of punk. Nevertheless, there was one important development that would subvert Mailer's seriousness and lead directly to the corrosive irony that has overtaken iconoclastic irony: the idea of "camp." First identified by Susan Sontag, camp was irony injected with a self-protecting and self-conscious aloofness and the utter refusal to take anything seriously. "Camp," wrote Sontag, is "the love of the exaggeration, the 'off,' the things-being-what-they-are-not . . . . camp sees everything in quotation marks." Where Mailer's essay on hip was a call to arms, camp was permission to giggle at authority and to treat all of life as a joke or, even better, theater—hence Sontag's critique of a film on the Army-McCarthy hearings not as history but as a play where "all the good guys come off bad." "Men used to rail at the irony of fate," Christopher Lasch wrote in *The Culture of Narcissism*, "now they prefer it to the irony of unceasing self-consciousness."

After the battles of the 1960s, it was this kind of ironic camp that became, and largely remains, the reigning ethos in our culture. David Letterman delivers the monologue behind a shield of smugness; rock musicians can't smile for fear of appearing human; and relationships between the sexes have become impossible to maintain. People, as Lasch noted, are afraid to feel. Compared with the *Men Are from Mars* psychobabble of today, the corny longing one sees while watching movies on the oldies cable television channel AMC, many of which feature swing bands, is bliss itself.

Predictably, the purveyors of rock culture just don't understand this—don't get that it is they who are now the conformists. (If everyone in your town is a polygamist, then monogamy becomes transgressive.) The most scathing and comprehensive indictment of swing came in late 1998, in the pages of *The Stranger*, a hip "alternative" paper in Seattle. "The Past Was Better Than the Present (And other Misconceptions of the Swing Movement)" is a dressing-down of nostalgia: "What does it mean that [young Americans] are fetishizing a period before rock and roll, before women's liberation, before Civil Rights?" asks writer Juliette Guilbert.

The answer? That kids these days are women-hating racists who wish Donna Reed was their girlfriend and Amos 'n' Andy were still on television. Guilbert equates the sharp-dressed Sinatra-worshipers of the 1990s to the blazer-and-tie conservatives she avoided on her college campus in the 1980s: "they are all wearing suits, the same tyrannous outfits their fathers fought and bled and wore bell bottoms to get away from." She then indulges in some ivory-tower hand-wringing: "Every level of our culture, from *Monday Night Football* to the *New Yorker* to people's choice of bathroom fixtures, reflects and inflects social structures and attitudes about things like—to cite the Big Three—race, class, and gender." And as such, the current nostalgia is deeply racist: when told by one martini-sipper that she liked the idea of "a time when we were all together," Guilbert snaps "The 'we' of this rose-tinted '40s and '50s included returning soldiers, pinup girls, housewives, bandleaders, the *Man in the Grey Flannel Suit*, bobbysoxers, greasers—but not blacks."

Say what you will about the new celebrants of America's cultural past, one thing that becomes clear after spending any time in the scene is that these people are not racists. They adore black culture, almost to a fault. They worship original lindy-hopper Frankie Manning, to say nothing of Ella Fitzgerald, Chick Webb, Duke Ellington, and other golden age giants. In fact, a few have made it their personal mission to see that these artists receive the honor today that racism made scarce while they were alive.

Guilbert acknowledges this—then offers an argument that reveals the deep racism of the left and liberal hacks like herself. Sure, she writes, these people love black jazz—but only as represented by the mindless bounce of dixieland and swing, the two earliest forms of jazz, and not the more esoteric and free-form bebop music of giants like the late sax legend John Coltrane. "When John Coltrane gets left out of retro, it's not just because you can't dance to his music, but because he was a black intellectual, and intellectuals cannot be portrayed as instinct-driven darkies who let go of intellect. As has happened so often in the past, black culture is made into a simple-minded inoculation against the disturbing complexities of modern life . . . it's a rebellion against the '60s." It is a rebellion against the 1960s, though not for the reasons she thinks.

Astonishly, Guilbert thinks the music of Duke Ellington and Louis Armstrong is not intellectual—as if the linear, Apollonian ride of a great swing chart is not more intelligent than the wilder Dionysian flights of bebop. But then, like all leftists, Guilbert sees blacks not as human beings but as aggrieved, radical political agents and measures their worth by how well they upset the applecart of bourgeois values. (Tellingly, critics like her never acknowledge that—if record sales are any indication—most blacks generally prefer the clean, candy-coated soul of a Whitney Houston to angry punk music or the black power militancy of Nation of Islam rappers Brand Nubian.) She also ignores the fact that most blacks, like those noble souls who once occupied the Secret City, are hard-working, church-going, conservative people. Like most liberals, Guilbert doesn't understand that we can go home again. It starts with a nice suit and a steady beat.

Index

A Note on the Author

Mark Gauvreau Judge, an award-winning journalist, is a contributing writer for the *New York Press*. His numerous articles on the arts and popular culture have appeared in the *Washington Post*, the *Weekly Standard*, *Salon*, the *New Criterion*, *First Things*, and other journals. He lives in Potomac, Maryland.

This book was designed and set into type

by Mitchell S. Muncy,

with cover design by FigDesign,

Irving, Texas,

and printed and bound

by Thomson-Shore, Inc.

Dexter, Michigan.

The text face is Minion,

designed by Robert Slimbach

and issued in digital form by Adobe Systems,

Mountain View, California, in 1991.

The paper is acid-free and is of archival quality.

26